CORRUPTION A SHORT HISTORY

A SHORT HISTORY

CORRUPTION

Carlo Alberto Brioschi

Translation by Antony Shugaar

BROOKINGS INSTITUTION PRESS
Washington, D.C.

The Brookings Institution is a private nonprofit organization devoted to research, education, and publication on important issues of domestic and foreign policy. Its principal purpose is to bring the highest quality independent research and analysis to bear on current and emerging policy problems. Interpretations or conclusions in Brookings publications should be understood to be solely those of the authors.

Library of Congress Cataloging-in-Publication data are available.

ISBN 978-0-8157-2791-0
ISBN 978-0-8157-2792-7

9 8 7 6 5 4 3 2 1

Typeset in Sabon

Composition by Westchester Publishing Services

CONTENTS

INTRODUCTION IF JULIUS CAESAR IS A THIEF

THE POLITICIAN'S CRAFT is commonly listed, along with prostitution, as one of the world's oldest professions. This longevity is no doubt largely attributable to the darker aspect of the political trade, that is, the realm of corruption, whose history is as long and twisted as that of mankind's attempt to live by the rule of law. Variously tolerated or fought, depending on time and place, the very definition of corruption has shifted frequently, as practitioners of corruption have encountered the ideas, laws, and customs of different peoples. Its essence, however, has remained unchanged. We can describe that essential core, as it appears in the political and administrative sphere on which we focus in this book, as the fraudulent behavior or actions of a public official willing to take money or gifts from vested interests or any other benefits in exchange for favors performed for or granted to the benefactor in question.

Who really cares, though, whether Julius Caesar is a thief? The question isn't a new one, but it hardly seems to have lost its relevance over the centuries: Few of us remember Demosthenes or Dante Alighieri for the cases in which they were accused of malfeasance; if anything, the impression is that the corruption of great men is considered practically inevitable. Perhaps this was due in part to the perception among the citizenry that by means of corruption they could count on a resulting increase in the general wealth, with greater opportunities for business or gifts for one and all. In other words, from the banquet table of the powerful crumbs might eventually make their way down to the level of the less mighty. "The national debt has, in fact, made more men rich than have a right to be so," wrote the poet Samuel Taylor Coleridge in the first half of the nineteenth century. "It is, in effect, like an ordinary, where three hundred tickets have been distributed, but where there is, in truth, room only for one hundred."[1]

Perhaps, then, the charges of conflict of interest and dishonesty leveled against the prince matter, and matter greatly, but it is not merely a matter of considerations of moralism and virtue. If the majority of a society's citizens in fact often vote into office a man or woman who offers unattainable dreams and illusory hopes, or if a great number of investors climb willingly onto the bandwagon of a captain of industry who is promising unlikely profits, we must try to gauge what real awareness the citizens have of the alleged dishonesty of their leaders and what real benefit can accrue to them from it: in other words, ascertain whether they don't particularly care, or whether a majority actually considers the malfeasance in question to be a significant and decisive *positive* factor at the moment they drop their ballots into the ballot box or as they make their way toward favor in the court of one in a succession of magnates. "Why did the people tolerate and even encourage and applaud these crimes?" wrote Elsa Morante in her considerations on fascist Italy under Benito Mussolini.[2] She answered her own question as follows: A part of the people did it "out of lack of moral awareness, a part out of cunning, a part out of self-interest or Machiavellianism," for, she says, "it is in the nature of the Italian people to vote for the strong man rather than the just man." For that matter, "It were as wise to oppose cyclones with discussion as the beliefs of crowds," as Gustave Le Bon wrote in his book *The Crowd: A Study of the Popular Mind.*[3]

There can be no doubt that hands stained with blood or filth still exercise a certain allure for common mortals, as long as a little gold dust is stuck to them too. Just as the Neros and the Caligulas have gone down in history every bit as often as the Christian saints (and far more often than the honest and undistinguished), so, too, the exploits of great scoundrels, as the nineteenth-century Scottish journalist and writer Charles Mackay tells us in his celebrated samplings of collective madness, tend to exert a powerful hold on the popular memory over the centuries. "Speculation is the romance of trade," Washington Irving wrote, "and casts contempt upon all its sober realities. It renders the stock-jobber a magician, and the exchange a region of enchantment."[4] Just to remain in the field of politics, without even having to delve very far into the past, we need only quote the late French President Charles de Gaulle when he observed that empires are not built by means of evangelical perfection. According to the French statesman, we should expect from empire builders massive doses of egotism as well as cunning—not always within the bounds of what is licit, understandably—but it is the results attained that will speak and win over the hearts of the people, transforming even defects into great qualities.

Now, since it is impossible to survey the minds of the collective with anything like reliable results, we might well limit ourselves to following the advice of Benedetto Croce, who tells us that it is not the historian's task to dwell upon "the details of the so-called bank scandals, and as to where lay the responsibility and the guilt. They provided a subject beloved of cheap moralists, and were made to serve the ends of the opponents of the Government. Business men of doubtful integrity, unscrupulous and unworthy politicians, fraudulent administrators, disloyal or corrupt officials, robbery on a small or a large scale, belong to all times and to all countries."[5] *Così fan tutti* (Everyone does it)—in other words, it's the way of the world, and the difference between good business and malfeasance is nothing more than a bribe, a payoff, an under-the-table tip. Why work oneself up if, in the end, the achievements attained by individuals in history outweigh the methods employed to bring them about, and even the underlying intentions? In short, what do we care if Napoleon was a greedy tyrant? He spread the principles of the French Revolution throughout Europe. Was his time in power also stained by cruelty? That is a matter deserving of the attention of a father confessor, not a historian. But if we fall into the habit of relativism, we'll be unable to distinguish throughout history between outright malfeasance and the most honest and unassailable behavior. And this honestly strikes us as a conceptual stretch likely to result in a very poor outcome. For example, the situation described by the Latin axiom that common error makes law: *Error communis facit jus*.

Lest we succumb to the temptation to overlook inherently minor cases of corruption that can still, however, ultimately result in serious violations, we might choose to approach the matter differently, namely, by seeking criteria for discrimination in the objective difference that exists between a large amount of malfeasance and a smaller quantity of the same (after all, as Diogenes Laertius suggested, "It is because of the great thieves that we hang the little thieves"). Agreed: A distinction between "enough is enough" and "a moderate violation" hardly seems like the stuff that makes for the highest level of judgment, but it does at least qualify as a first criterion of distinction. We are not talking about legitimate offerings and patronage, legal lobbying or spoils, and legitimate forms of reciprocity, but about public officials' conflicts of interests and bribery: "payments" in the form of cronyism, opportunities for embezzling, nepotism, extortion, tips, gifts, sops, perks, skims, advantages, discounts, kickbacks, funding, influence peddling, inflated sale prices, stock options, secret commissions, or promotion (rise in rank). There is of course a scale in the gravity of these crimes and misdemeanors, but there is no distinguishing between bad and "honest graft"—an argument put forth by George W. Plunkitt, a member of New York's Tammany Hall machine.

In this book I trace the overarching outlines, the historic fault lines of the phenomenon of corruption, and while doing so I cleave to the narrower issue of the corruption of "public officials." By so doing, once I have clearly defined and laid out a proper perspective, it will become easier to explore the centuries in Western history and culture as well as to highlight the pliability of the powerful and the less powerful in the face of illicit offers and the temptations of their subordinates, in particular with respect to the kind of potential corner cutting that skirts the requirements of the norm.

I shall review the corrupt exploits and customs of the great and the mediocre, focusing among their ranks upon rulers, politicians, judges, and the numerous financial con men, both real and fictional. I shall also focus on those who wrote about them, likewise important witnesses for the simple fact that they took on the topic of the contradictions of human greed. Mine is a more or less chronological itinerary, one that is for the most part Occidental, concentrating on European and American history. This because, as is evident, corruption is a social and cultural phenomenon, as well as a political one, and it ought to be investigated in the most homogeneous context possible in order to identify its distinguishing traits as well as the crucial turning points in its history. It is this last point that constitutes the objective, however modest, of this overview.

By turning points I am referring to those moments in which corruption managed to switch masks, thanks to an individual, a political movement, or certain social mores, and burrow ever deeper into the ordinary conduct of power. I am, of course, well aware that the Western world hardly constitutes the world at large, but it remains the world that I know, the world in which I am immersed. I shall therefore draw not only on history and the more everyday accounts of events past, but also on a wide variety of publications of a philosophical, political, sociological, and normative nature, as well as on the literary, dramatic, pictorial, and cinematic documentation of different eras, which often provide a fascinating mirror of the times that engendered them.

Tracing a historical trajectory of corruption can, in fact, prove useful, not so much to document its ineradicable nature as, rather, to understand corruption's characteristics, mechanisms, and effects in certain crucial periods and times of transition. Thus, we can abandon the conditioned reflex of minimal or muted reaction that generally comes over us when confronted with the continuous succession of scandals that fill the daily press—ranging from the collapse of Lehman Brothers (the largest financial collapse in the history of the United States) to the scandal involving FIFA, the international soccer federation, in its process of assigning countries world soccer championships; from Iraqgate to the investigation into Volkswagen's emissions scandal—a reaction that is frequently limited to a feeling of helpless indignation or apathetic disinterest.

Anthropology teaches that all individuals tend to adapt to the social conventions that characterize the culture to which they belong. Each of us speaks the language we hear spoken, and it is only with great difficulty that any of us rejects the forms of behavior that are established as customs. Likewise, corruption can appear to us as an accepted standard simply because it is practiced on a widespread basis in the environment to which we belong. And in that environment, the name and the nature of corruption can be two very different things, just as the degrees of rejection or, conversely, social acceptance of corruption itself can vary widely. For instance, the ancient Egyptians, in order to describe a phenomenon distinct from corruption but still related to it, such as the "offering," spoke of *feqa*, while the Mesopotamians spoke of *tatu*, the Bible mentions *shohadh*, the Greeks call it *doron*, and the Latins *munus*. In each case reference is to a gift that is by no means entirely inconsequential, an offering that is seen as compensation for the satisfaction of a legitimate interest (or the expectation of the same). In the present day, the French refer to bribes as *pots de vin*, thus suggesting the natural and inevitable origin of a tip meant to grease the wheels of a machine that operates chaotically at best. In English both *bribe* and *sleaze* are common terms, while the German word for corrupting someone is *bestechen* (from *stechen*, "to sting; to stab") or else *schmieren* (from *Schmiere*, "grease, oil"), hence the corresponding term for bribe: *Schmiergeld* (literally, "grease money"). It is no accident that many believe that a country first begins to corrupt itself beginning with its syntax, and the use of euphemistic locutions to spin a web of vagueness around a phenomenon for which a single word would surely suffice offers the clearest of confirmations.

But what has genuinely changed over the course of history has been the very concept of corruption, oscillating between the configuration of a generic moral decadence on the part of a political and social body, clear evidence of an effort to harness the consensus that is linked and intrinsic to power itself, as well as the stigmatization of a veritable "abuse of public office," the term that has come to be accepted in modern times. In antiquity, "greasing the wheels" was as widespread a custom as it is today, but it was in some cases considered perfectly legitimate. In the Old Testament, we meet judges and rulers who direct lavish efforts toward the benefit of the most generous and munificent among their subjects. The trading of favors, and the reciprocity that underlies the relationship involved, were at the very least tolerated. Where there was a perception of wrongdoing, it had to do not with the act of a vested interest making a gift, but rather with the abandonment of the logic inherent in the exchange, that is, a failure to give value in exchange for an offering received. The Bible itself, in particular the Pentateuch, seems to offer streaks of testimony to the social diffusion of the practice of *do ut des* ("I give, so that you may give," much the same as a quid pro quo): After all, we might reasonably view Moses, adviser to Pharaoh, as a beneficiary of friends in high places and the methods that Moses uses to persuade the sovereign to let his people go as a clear case of extortion and intimidation (although the idea of divine intervention surely makes this interpretation somewhat sacrilegious). The idea of corruption as a sin and an absolute moral fault emerges in the New Testament, where we find a public denunciation of the emblematic episode of the "generous" Simon Magus, who was ready to offer cash in order to acquire the powers conferred by the Holy Spirit. It is no accident that this individual lends his name to a practice, simony, that would for many centuries constitute, so to speak, the ecclesiastic version of corruption and would eventually contribute to the explosion of the Protestant Reformation.

In his book *Power and Prosperity: Outgrowing Communist and Capitalist Dictatorships*, the American economist and social scientist Mancur Olson (1932–1938) distinguishes between "roving bandits," who emerge in anarchic situations and are only interested in stealing and destruction, and "stationary bandits": the first tyrants, who are interested in the economic growth of their lands only as long as they can remain in power and can benefit from it. That is why they begin to develop some government functions and try to protect their citizens and properties from the depredations of roving bandits. In Olson's view, the evolution from roving to stationary bandits can be considered the beginning of civilization, and the seed of the later form of government called democracy.

Corruption was commonly practiced in the Greek polis of the fifth century, known as the cradle of democracy. In courts of law, the jurors, chosen by drawing lots, were often willing to sell their votes. For that matter, centuries earlier, in the Archaic Age, Homer stated that it is a deplorable act to turn down a gift and explains in his works how it was possible in a certain sense to "buy" even divine protection. The greatest Greek poet seems to teach in *The Odyssey* that one should never appear in a royal or aristocratic court without an offer in hand, and that, conversely, "it is not well to refuse a gift."[6] In *The Iliad* it is clear that even the favor of the gods can be propitiated through the bestowal of gifts and the right offerings:

They ranged the holy hecatomb all orderly round the altar of the god. They washed their hands and took up the barley-meal to sprinkle over the victims, while Chryses lifted up his hands and prayed aloud on their behalf. "Hear me," he cried, "O god of the silver bow, that protectest Chryse and holy Cilla, and rulest Tenedos with thy might. Even as thou didst hear me aforetime when I prayed, and didst press hardly upon the Achaeans, so hear me yet again, and stay this fearful pestilence from the Danaans." Thus did he pray, and Apollo heard his prayer.[7]

There were of course laws in Athens to punish those who accepted earnings for private interest to the detriment of the collective interest, but it is worth remembering that within the general social context those interests included slavery and clientelism and a political system that called for unpaid public office, which certainly did little to incentivize proper conduct on the part of the officeholders.

The word "corruption" first bursts onto the scene in ancient Rome—the term in fact takes its origin from the Latin *corrumpere*, which meant, in legal language, the manumission of a judicial document in exchange for compensation and, in a broader sense, an unhealthy action, a system in deterioration and slipping into decay (a metaphor that would spread spectacularly, that of the social and political body which, like a human body rotting, undergoes the decay of its organs and a slow ensuing dissolution). In Rome the phenomenon of electoral corruption was given a very specific name: *ambitus*, and it spread especially during the republican age, the unmistakable demonstration that it was not only the monarchic form of government that encouraged dishonest behavior and acts of corruption, as Cicero (106–43 B.C.) claimed when he condemned the autarchic regimes of Sulla and Caesar.

The High Middle Ages (ca. 1001–1300) did not witness the establishment of a specific notion of political corruption. As we shall see, the changed social conditions played their role in conveying the element of corruption into a broader configuration of man's moral, spiritual, and corporeal vices, unleashed upon the world as a consequence of Adam's original sin—this was the picture of corruption offered by Saint Paul. This of course doesn't mean that the phenomenon itself experienced in that period any form of contraction. In fact, the feudal system intrinsically called for a form of protection on the part of the powerful, extended toward the weaker members of society, from the highest level to the lowest, that brought with it requests, obligations, and continuous exchanges among the actors involved, in confirmation of a practice that we might nowadays call patronage.

Historians have identified one particular period, the Early Middle Ages, between the fifth and tenth centuries, during which an economic system came into being that was based on an exchange corresponding to a social bond "legalized in custom if not in public documents." Starting in the eleventh century, however, a mindset spread that was bound up with profit and could be termed commercial, as we understand the term today. But the true shift in economic and social relations and in the practice of favor-trading came around the middle of the 1300s, when a rapid economic transformation witnessed the consolidation of the coin as an instrument for the payment of goods and services and as a medium of exchange. Its spread was facilitated by such calamitous events as the outbreaks of the plague that so tragically ravaged vast swathes of Europe. Beginning with this event, so central to the history of man, the exchange of goods and favors could begin to take concrete form and crystallize into the exchange of cash as we now know it. Thus corruption, too, marked the dawn of modernity.

In Dante's *Divine Comedy* (written between 1308 and 1320), that corruption thus conceived is openly stigmatized with the term of *baratteria*—the secular version of simony—especially in reference to holders of public office who are suborned and then involved in dishonest actions. These forms of behavior did not represent merely an offense to God, but also a full-fledged betrayal of the trust of the citizenry as well as the public mission with which they had been entrusted. Among the characters that Dante places between the sixth and ninth circles of Hell are Fra Gomita, a notable citizen of Pisa, and Michele Zanche, governor of Sardinia, well known for the bribes he extorted. They are being punished not only for the wrongs they committed but also for what befell their communities as a result of their actions. Thus, they find themselves in the fiery infernal chaos of the city of Dis, which they themselves seem to have helped to bring down into ruin through their own conduct.

Later we begin to see an abandonment of the Christian conception of spiritual corruption and the accompanying physical deterioration of the social body as a whole, with, for instance, the work of Marsilius of Padua, one of the first to uphold the necessity of a separation of powers, and essentially the separation of secular power from religious power, including where malfeasance was concerned. Marsilius identified a case of the distortion of the duties of a public official and went so far as to consider an even more serious matter the corruption of the clergy (with a view in particular to the interested distribution of ecclesiastical positions and indulgences) than the corruption of the prince: in the latter case sleaze dies with the sovereign, whereas the fruit of the former is destined to endure for all eternity.

Fifteenth-century Venice saw the institutionalization and justification of the *broglio*: the term was originally used to describe the public trade of citizens' votes to whoever made the highest offer, in effect, an auction that was held in front of the Doge's Palace. Later *broglio* came to mean a competition for public offices using cash bids, and it finally came to be synonymous with political corruption understood more broadly. But the first writer to condemn and clearly define *broglio* as the antithesis of civic virtue and as a political problem more than a spiritual one was the Florentine thinker Niccolò Machiavelli. Only later followed simplistic interpretations that have linked his thought to the idea that the ends justify the means.

Subsequently, the Protestant Reformation, with its explicit condemnation of corruption in the heart of the Roman Catholic Church, helped to separate the practice of simony from the civil buying and selling of the favors of public officials. It was a transition that would only be completed with the revolution in commerce and the first industrial age, a period that saw the growth of conflicts of interest between rulers and entrepreneurs. As a result, it became clear that greater regulation of business, trade and initiatives of free enterprise was needed. In that period a modern conception of corruption as a crime developed on the part of those who hold public office, a full-fledged legal infraction, clearly distinct from any strictly moral evaluation and the concept of "sin."

This separation was as crucial as the separation of church and state—it is perhaps no accident that the concept of ethical finance is presented today as one of the ethical strong points of Islam, which tends to resist such separation. In the field we are studying, the fruits of the separation ripened slowly, but ripen they did, and at a certain point, something started to change. We are now talking about the eighteenth century, during the time of the greatest flowering of philosophy as well as the triumphant rise of trade and commerce, and in particular of the British Empire. While Daniel Defoe in his *Free-Holder's Plea Against Stock-jobbing Elections of Parliament Men*, printed in 1701, denounced the growing corruption of parliament, which he felt was detrimental to the welfare of the nation and the citizenry, the prime minister, Robert Walpole, was effectively accused of illicit speculation during the notorious South Sea Bubble, a collapse that left thousands of small investors penniless. The charges leveled at him by Lord Bolingbroke had to do, among other things, with a broader network of vote buying, a bustling market in parliamentary offices and positions, and the distribution of privileges in exchange for loyalty and favors. Those charges failed to hold up in court. Political corruption was by this point a deep-rooted reality, and its supporters began to make their voices heard. These were the years in which we begin to see the work of proponents of the necessity of payoffs, such as Bernard de Mandeville writing in *The Fable of the Bees: Or, Private Vices, Publick Benefits* (1705), as well as "new realists" such as David Hume and Adam Smith. In their thinking the quest for profit was entirely rehabilitated and the attainment of personal interest was recognized as a lever promoting the material and social progress of the citizenry.

Something had changed. Corruption was no longer simply an immoral consequence of economic success, luxury, and decadence. The old classical and Christian model spiraled into crisis; it seemed incapable of standing up to the economic progress of a society in the midst of rapid transformation, what with a demographic revolution, new relations between the sovereign and Parliament, an increase in trade, and the need for rules and security that only a centralized state could attempt to institute. This led to the consolidation of a narrower concept of corruption: crime strictly understood as the violation of a specific law of the state. At the same time, a sort of renunciation of moral condemnation, with no ifs, ands, or buts, seems to indicate that by this point corruption was considered to a be an endemic disease: a phenomenon to be combated—if necessary with hair-of-the-dog remedies, such as small doses of corruption itself—even in the full awareness that the fight could never entirely be won.

Precisely at this point in history those who had already rejected on a wholesale basis this realpolitik development in the Old World, with all the accompanying cynicism we might expect, decided to cut all ties with the past and set out to found a new order in the New World. In the eighteenth century the United States achieved its independence from England, rejecting its forms of government and, with them, its corrupt political customs. British officials who held positions of power in the North American colonies had often given proof of their abilities to wring personal profit and bribes with practices that verged on extortion. One estimate made in 1765 of the losses to the British treasury that were due to the corruption of colonial functionaries was £700,000 (almost $1.8 million in 2017 dollars). Benjamin Fletcher (1640–1703), governor of the English colony in New York, was investigated and removed from office in 1697 by the British Lords of Trade. He was found guilty of having negotiated with pirates to ensure his ships would make it safe to port in exchange for bribes.

The very Constitution of the new United States was drafted with the unmistakable concern on the part of the Founding Fathers that the ruling class of the new nation not fall into the tragic error of a dangerous conflict between public and private interests. In spite of this, and despite the subsequent periods marked by such moralizing presidencies as those of James Monroe (in office 1817–1825) and Theodore Roosevelt (in office 1901–1909), the phenomenon of corruption never failed to spread vigorously and tirelessly in the New World. The topic remains the topic of lively discussion, in particular with respect to the intricate issue of private finance in politics, election campaigns, the power of lobbyists, and the legislative actions of politicians thus benefited. Meanwhile, in the Old World, the bureaucracies of the nineteenth century and the dictatorships of the twentieth century opened new chapters of the old book, injecting new vigor into an ancient phenomenon. Today we less see bribes in the form of money passing from one hand to the other but finance and politics remain strictly tied, albeit in a far more sophisticated fashion, and the conflicts of interest of our rulers is still a problem that must be combatted globally (a larger problem in some countries than others as we learn from the annual Transparency International's perception of corruption index). For example, in the 2016 American presidential election, both of the two principal candidates, Donald Trump and Hillary Clinton, were accused of fraud and various types of corruption.

Mark E. Warren argues that the essence of corruption in a democracy is "duplicitous exclusion": many citizens in democracies feel excluded from decisions that affect their lives because of wealth inequalities and fully legal processes that nonetheless reinforce those advantages. We can see the consequences in the electoral and political trends of a growing number of countries that warn us to be aware of the corruption dimensions of populist discontent.[8]

From the rapid review of the centuries offered here—we shall examine them in greater detail in the chapters that follow—we can glimpse a sort of cyclical process. At the high points of malfeasance, where there is no concealing the spread and the sheer volume of the theft and the impunity of the political class, efforts frequently emerge—or at least the appearance thereof—to bring about reform in order to stem the practice of bribe taking. For every Verres (120–43 B.C.), a corrupt governor of Sicily when it was a wealthy province of the Roman Empire, there was always a Cicero ready to condemn his misdeeds. The thefts of Caesar were opposed by Metellus; Martin Luther rose up in protest in the face of the excesses of Pope Leo X's clientelism. Every thief (of whatever rank and nature) has come up against an adversary with various degrees of success or failure for each. The conservative historian Edmund Burke fought against the misdeeds of Warren Hastings, the first governor of the British East Indies; Felice Cavallotti shot his darts against the murky business of Italy's Francesco Crispi government (1887–1901); the Socialist Giacomo Matteotti (1885–1924) raised his voice in the Italian parliament against Mussolini.

The battle for political power often makes use of the crowbar of politically motivated or legal accusations against the corrupt nature of the ruler or leader. The method may appear rather unorthodox, but in this way the mechanism of alternating parties in power tends to work more efficiently, provided that there is always a political party cut out of the division of the political spoils and interested in change, and at least some element of the institutions of the media willing to play the role of "guard dog of democracy." Thomas Carlyle observed that "a Great Man, we said, was always sincere, as the first condition of him. But a man need not be great in order to be sincere; that is not the necessity of Nature and of all Time, but only of certain corrupt unfortunate epochs of Time."[9] That is to say, the epochs in which the ideas set forth by Bernard de Mandeville in the eighteenth century seem to prevail, the periods when, as he pointed out in his *Fable of the Bees*, corruption is the true engine driving the world, where progress is impossible without it.

In any case, although the philosopher Benedetto Croce surely had a point when he maintained that history pays no mind to ordinary everyday pilfering, it is every bit as true that bribery in politics, in all its various manifestations, has had an enormous impact on the economies of every nation and their inhabitants, in some cases producing significant effects on the gross domestic product, the state of welfare, and the daily lives of the citizenry, and thus threatening to affect the fate of a nation, not only over the short term but over the long term as well.

That is why taking on the daunting challenge of a history of corruption, which could potentially be an endless task, not only constitutes an exercise in academic reconstruction but can also prove useful in exploring the question of malfeasance nowadays, in the context of the longer term. We thus emerge from the mere conditioned reflex of indignation, which generally takes over in the face of current scandals—and just as quickly flickers and dies out—and are able to sketch out future prospects of safeguarding our social entity and ultimately the collective welfare with greater understanding. We know that if, over the centuries, the protean force of corruption has taken on ever new forms and features—and it has—new, inventive ways of fighting it have also always been found and put into practice, and we can improve on them. Acts of corruption can be thwarted only if we use to maximum effect fundamental tools such as an efficient system of justice, a genuinely free process of reporting the news, and strict respect for the principle of accountability in every act of administration.

ONE THE GIFT IN ANTIQUITY

Exchange, Favor, and Sacrifice,
from Hammurabi to the Bible

KAUṬILYA, A BRAHMIN in the fourth century B.C., known also as Chanakya, who was minister to the Indian king Chandragupta Maurya, wrote a fascinating book on the art of government entitled *Arthashastra*, which might be translated as "Instructions on Material Prosperity." The Indian economist Amartya Sen has suggested a simpler translation: "Economics." The Sanskrit text, discovered in 1905, also explores the vast and evergreen phenomenon of corruption.

According to Kauṭilya, a contemporary of Aristotle, those who govern must use every means to attain their objectives; rules of rigor and honesty seem to apply, at least in substance, only to their subjects. This message ultimately aligns Kauṭilya with Machiavelli, in spite of the considerable distance in time between the two men and the different historical contexts in which they lived and wrote. Among Kauṭilya's adages, the best known may be the one about how difficult it is to prove the financial dishonesty of a public official. "Just as fish moving under water cannot possibly be found out either as drinking or not drinking water, so government servants employed in government work cannot be found out [while] taking money [for themselves]." He noted in the *Arthashastra*, "Just as it is impossible not to taste the honey or the poison that finds itself at the tip of the tongue, so it is impossible for a government servant not to eat up, at least a bit of the king's revenue."[1]

In antiquity, greasing the wheels was a custom every bit as widespread as it is today, but it was not always condemned. Basically a religious practice such as sacrifice constitutes, with all the distinctions and caveats that we might apply to a ritual and its attendant symbolisms, a form of quid pro quo. The message that is transmitted— through the hierarchies of the religious caste, to be sure— is that the deity or deities are more likely to smile upon the rich man, who can afford to immolate valuable livestock, than upon the poor man. In the Old Testament judges and rulers turn their favor to the most forthcoming of their subjects: cunning zealots, willing to spend profuse amounts of money and immolate sacrificial victims. The trading of favors, and the necessary reciprocity underlying that relationship, are not only tolerated and admitted—they are even regulated and formalized. Cutting partially in the opposite direction is an equally ancient concept, namely that of the Jubilee, the year in which all debts and all contracts are dissolved and forgiven. But that tangent would take us too far afield, in part because sacrifice, favor, and corruption are concepts that we must keep quite separate, particularly in a historic and symbolic universe that possesses codes of behavior and rituals that are profoundly different from our own.

On the less slippery terrain of human, not divine, affairs, Hammurabi, one of the most celebrated lawmakers of the ancient world, wrote that a judge should be expelled from his post if he changed a verdict that had already been sealed. There is no evidence that this was a specific reaction on Hammurabi's part to verdicts that had been changed in return for a payoff to solve a situation, so we cannot say whether this was a measure intended to prevent cases of the corruption of judges. It is possible, instead, that the punishment had to do with verdicts not applied or even cases of judges who had not done their part in exchange for a gift. In fact, not only was the custom of gift giving widespread, but there might even be an express condemnation of the reverse customs—failure to offer a gift, or of a judge's refusal of a gift.

In ancient Mesopotamia, Gimil-Ninurta, a poor but free man and a citizen of Nippur, seeks to improve his lot. All he has is his goat. Leading the goat by his left hand, he brings it to the residence of the mayor, and is made to wait. But when the mayor hears that he has something to offer he is indignant at his slaves. A citizen of Nippur, he says, should be admitted promptly. He sends for Gimil-Ninurta and asks, "What is your problem that you bring me an offering?" Gimil-Ninurta says nothing but greets him with his right hand, invokes blessings on him, and gives him the goat. The mayor announces he will hold a feast. But when the feast is held, all that Gimil-Ninurta receives is a bone and a sinew of the goat and stale beer. He asks the meaning of such treatment. In reply he is beaten on the mayor's orders. He departs, vowing vengeance. Later, Gimil-Ninurta visits the king of the entire country and offers him one mina of gold in return for the use of the royal chariot for a day. The king asks no questions but agrees at once. In the chariot Gimil-Ninurta returns to Nippur, where the mayor receives him as a high official of the realm. Installed in the mayor's residence, he secretly opens the chest he has brought and pretends the gold he says was in it has disappeared. He implies that the mayor is guilty of stealing it and gives the mayor three beatings for his crime. The mayor also placates him with a gift of two minas of gold.[2]

This story, which appears in *Bribes*, by John Thomas Noonan—one of the few authors who has attempted to explore in a thorough and diachronic manner the topic of political corruption over the centuries—and is known by the title "The Poor Man of Nippur," probably dates from 1500 B.C. It shows how among the peoples of ancient Mesopotamia the law of reciprocity—the natural rule of quid pro quo—was strictly respected, whereas any wandering from the straight and narrow path was punished. The misdeed lay not in the act of making an interested gift but rather in breaking with the logic of the exchange: in failing to offer value in exchange for value received.

Noonan comments that the most serious misdeed lay not in the act of corrupting but in the effect of corruption: breaking one's word in a society where keeping one's word was considered to be a divine characteristic. He cites in this connection a fragment of a hymn to the sun god Shamash, preserved in the library of Ashurbanipal in Nineveh, where we can read the following phrase: "Your manifest utterance may not be changed."[3] The word *tatu* used in the text of Hammurabi, in a section titled "The Corrupt Judge," generically indicates the offering of a subordinate. Offering and corruption therefore trail off one into the other, and a more generalized condemnation of corrupt giving will only arrive later, in the modern age, even while the practice of exchange will in any case remain a constant custom.

A bright thread runs between corruption, profferings, and sacrifices, and it handsomely bears investigation because we should naturally distinguish between customs and usages, although the underlying perception may be nothing more than a mere matter of nuance. A substantial portion of the revenue of the priestly caste unquestionably came from offerings. In the ancient sanctuary of Shiloh, during the sacrifices, the priests had a right to everything that a "flesh hook of three teeth" could take (I Samuel 2:13–15). Evidently, when meeting with prophets you should never show up empty-handed. That is why, in I Samuel 9:7, Saul hesitates to approach Samuel to seek advice; to the servant who suggests he do so, he explains, "But, behold, if we go, what shall we bring the man? For the bread is spent in our vessels, and there is not a present to bring to the man of God: what have we?" The servant reassures Saul and offers the fourth part of a shekel of silver that he has with him for Saul to offer to Samuel. In Genesis (28:20–22), Jacob does not hesitate to propose a deal with the Almighty, a sort of daring contract with the

Lord: "If God will be with me, and will keep me in this way that I go, and will give me bread to eat, and raiment to put on, So that I come again to my father's house in peace; then shall the Lord be my God: And this stone, which I have set for a pillar, shall be God's house: and of all that thou shalt give me I will surely give the tenth unto thee."

In short, it is no accident that Delilah, corrupted by the Philistines to get the secret of Samson's strength, is not entirely depicted as a negative figure, but if anything as a cunning and skillful woman. The Old Testament of course does not advocate the idea of corruption established as a system. Among the instructions that God gives Moses is this: "And thou shalt take no gift: for the gift blindeth the wise, and perverteth the words of the righteous" (Exodus 23:8). The Lord does not accept offerings from those who are unworthy, but only from a man whom He deems just. All the same, the principle of exchange, of the reciprocity of relations between men and their God, still permeates much of the sacred scriptures. The ancient society of the Middle East as mirrored in the Old Testament appears to be informed by this principle.

Things change in the New Testament, where a logic of the freely given, or at least a different way of calculating "favors," comes to the fore. Let us recall one of the most famous of Jesus's parables, that of the poor widow and her miserable offering to the treasury of the Temple. At the same time there is a public denunciation of the emblematic episode of the "generous" Simon Magus, ready to offer cash to acquire the powers conferred by the Holy Spirit. When Simon saw Peter and John come from Jerusalem to baptize a number of converts like him, and "saw that through laying on of the apostles' hands the Holy Ghost was given, he offered them money, saying, give me also this power, that on whomsoever I lay hands, he may receive the Holy Ghost" (Acts 8:18–19)—words that cost him a harsh accusation from Peter and an extraordinary posthumous celebrity. This episode is the origin of the concept of simony, the buying or selling of a church office or preferment, which is, so to speak, the ecclesiastical version of corruption and which for many centuries the church would continue to condemn—or at least pay lip service to that condemnation—while largely tolerating it until the practice prompted the outraged denunciation of Martin Luther.

We cannot forget, for that matter, that there was an offer of cash at the heart of one of the central episodes of all Christian history, the corruption of Judas Iscariot, the man who held the disciples' money and who sold his master, Jesus, to the Romans for thirty pieces of silver—a betrayal so rife with consequences that for Judas, in the Christian tradition, there is no redemption.

But an examination of the correlation between corruption and betrayal—especially in a context as dense with meaning as the evangelical setting—would only take us away from our chosen topic, that of politics. Instead, to stay on topic, it is interesting to see what happens in the political heart of the much celebrated cradle of democracy: Athens.

TWO DEMOCRACY AND DECADENCE

Corruption and Political Buying and Selling in Ancient Greece

A NEW OLYMPIAD began in Athens in 324 B.C., and that same year the scandal of Harpalus's gold erupted. Demosthenes, renowned for his orations against Philip II of Macedon, was accused of having taken possession of the sums deposited on the Acropolis by Alexander's treasurer. Demosthenes was convicted and had to flee. This is certainly one of the best known scandals of ancient Greece. And, in fact, Demosthenes, after returning to Athens from forced exile, ultimately died a suicide, bequeathing to posterity this motto: "Envy toward him whom gold has seduced; jests and laughter if he confesses it; pardon if he is convicted; hatred against his accuser."[1]

The problem of corruption had been explored much earlier by Hesiod (active ca. 750–650 B.C.), who had in his poetry celebrated a mythical golden age. But the "invention" of democracy was not destined to eradicate corruptive practices, and in the Greek polis of the fifth century, corruption and demagogy went hand in hand. In the courts of law, the jurors, chosen by lot, were willing to sell their votes. Plato writes in *The Republic* that the guardians of the state shall never even be allowed to deal with money: "To them alone, out of the city's population, it is forbidden to handle or touch gold or silver, or be beneath the same roof, or wear it as jewelry, or drink from gold or silver cups. In this way they will be kept safe, and they will keep the city safe."[2] But that it was anything but realistic to think that public functionaries might display such nobility of spirit appears evident from the words that Plato puts in Socrates's mouth: "For I am certain, O men of Athens, that if I had engaged in politics, I should have perished long ago. . . . No man who goes to war with you or any other multitude, honestly striving against the many lawless and unrighteous deeds which are done in a state, will save his life."[3]

Is it really impossible then to govern without doing harm and triggering discontent?

Aristotle, in the *Nicomachean Ethics*, describes the despot as someone who pursues his own interest in the context of a tyrannical, oligarchic, or demagogic system, although he does add that a good man must in a certain sense be "selfish," because that is the only way he will be able to help either himself or the community. In other words, mind one's own business while also tending to the business of others. And perhaps this is why, even then, the first to arouse suspicion was the man who leveled the accusation, sometimes even before and to an even greater extent than the accused. He was thought to conceal, with greater or lesser degrees of cunning, a personal interest in making public his accusation instead of preserving a lower profile. Not without reason. In the Greek polis, where the office of public prosecutor could be performed without distinction by any and all citizens, the sycophants often worked in concert to procure sources of income by making accusations with varying levels of foundation in fact, or else by assuring silence on certain matters they had come to be aware of. Demosthenes offers this description of the professional calumniator: "He makes his way through the market-place like a snake or a scorpion with sting erect, darting hither and thither, on the lookout for someone on whom he can call down disaster or calumny or mischief of some sort, or whom he can terrify till he extorts money from him."[4]

Western political philosophy—beginning with Plato and his disciples, who were supporters of the intimate bond between ethics and politics, as well as of the abolition of private property (considered an undeniable source of corruption)—has always theorized the "despotic instinct" of power: man's natural propensity to use whatever power he possesses to further his own specific interests. The orator and sophist Thrasymachus, who lived in the fifth century B.C., is known today chiefly because Plato made him the protagonist of one of his dialogues. Thrasymachus stated, "I proclaim that justice is nothing else than the interest of the stronger."[5] In other words, justice need not simply be pursued in respect for the rules underlying the order of the community; justice can be constructed artfully in accordance with the needs of the ruler. Those who govern, then, can make laws that guarantee their own impunity.

Plato's tale of his relation to politics traces a perfect parable. From an early age, he writes, he was inclined toward politics, with some delusions to play the part of a moralizer. Socrates's arrest–on what Plato calls "a most iniquitous charge"—trial, and death were a turning point of sorts. From then on, politics would seem to him a murkier and murkier affair:

> The farther I advanced in life, the more difficult it seemed to me to handle public affairs aright. For it was not possible to be active in politics without friends and trustworthy supporters; and to find these ready to my hand was not an easy matter, since public affairs at Athens were not carried on in accordance with the manners and practices of our fathers; nor was there any ready method by which I could make new friends. The laws too, written and unwritten, were being altered for the worse, and the evil was growing with startling rapidity.

Plato's attempts at winning back his earlier fascination with politics don't achieve any result but the discovery, sooner or later, of more misbehavior. "Finally, it became clear to me, with regard to all existing communities, that they were one and all misgoverned. For their laws have got into a state that is almost incurable, except by some extraordinary reform with good luck to support it."

This has a final ring to it, but it must be remembered that Plato actually puts forward a possible remedy for corruption and injustice: philosophy. "Either those who are pursuing a right and true philosophy receive sovereign power in the States, or those in power in the States by some dispensation of providence become true philosophers."[6] Why philosophers? For many reasons, certainly, but for one in particular: The philosopher is the man who by definition ought to be most capable of discerning good, as he is more interested in moral questions than material ones, such as wealth.

In Greek tragedy and comedy, the theme of corruption and, more generally, its relationship with wealth (leaving aside the issues of its possible provenance) is recurrent and central. "Wealth, sovereignty and skill outmatching skill for the contrivance of an envied life!" Sophocles has Oedipus say in *Oedipus the King*. "Great store of jealousy fills your treasury chests, if my friend Creon, friend from the first and loyal, thus secretely attacks me, secretely desires to drive me out and secretely suborns this juggling, trick devising quack, this wily beggar who has only eyes for his own gains, but blindness in his skill."[7]

In comedy, on the other hand, we find the figure of Paphlagon, a corrupt and powerful man, a protagonist of Aristophanes's *The Knights*. The people denounce his actions in a series of taunts: "God bless me, bursting with good cheer!" "That fish cake too! Why, most of it's still here. For me he cut a little slice, no more." "That's just the way he treated you before. He doled you out small bits of what he got and kept the big things for his private pot." "Rogue, with your thieving how you did me down, 'Me, who bestowed thy riches and thy crown.'" And Paphlagon, confused, responds, "I only stole things for my country's good."[8]

The example is perfect, in the past and in the present: often political leaders in the present day, when caught up in financial scandals, have claimed that they were stealing for the party, or for the cause, and in any case for some higher good. As if leaders, secretaries, treasurers, local councilmen, and members of parliament didn't draw some more or less direct advantage from the system of finance that allows them to get elected. The Greek historian Plutarch (A.D. 45–120), who compared the great and the good of the Greek and Roman worlds in his *Parallel Lives* and lamented the corruption of the Greek world, left us a wealth of fragments collected under the title *Moralia*, which shows how keen he was to instruct his contemporaries—and posterity. In his *Life of Themistocles* he tells a revealing anecdote about the great Athenian general. Standing by the sea after the battle of Salamis, Themistocles saw many corpses washed up on the shore. There were riches too, bracelets and ornaments. He did not touch a thing, but he told his friend, "Take you these things, for you are not Themistocles."[9] The story does not reveal what his friend made of this not-too-veiled insult, but Plato's idea that leaders should avoid acquiring riches is clearly still at work here.

And so, in the rich cultural and philosophical climate of ancient Greece a commonplace took shape that wasn't new then and was destined to exert an influence that it has not lost even today: the relationship between luxury and decadence, of course with a strong element of corruption and vested interests. A people that is too rich is a people weakened, incapable of great things. And the same can be said of that people's leaders, if it is true that often one of the most highly acclaimed characteristics of many acknowledged great men is a frugality that verges on asceticism (whether real or presumed).

Of the general Callicratidas, an authentic symbol of Spartan rigor who died heroically in a naval battle in 405 B.C., it is said that when he was in great need of money for himself and for his army, he turned down fifty thousand minas offered to him in exchange for a favor, saying curtly, "I won't sell myself for an unjust cause." "If I'd been Callicratidas, I'd have accepted," Cleander, one of his officers, said to him. And the general replied, harshly, "So would I, if I'd been Cleander."[10] An opposing conception, we might say, to that set forth by the French philosopher Michel Onfray (b. 1959), who revived and updated, with some success, the thoughts of the Greek cynics, from Antisthenes to Crates of Thebes, proclaiming the necessity of reviving those pitiless truths in order to defend oneself from the domesticated thought of an era in which hypocrisy holds sway. His idea is that we must go "toward a wisdom without morality," as promised in one of his most celebrated books, *Cosmos*.[11]

Jacob Burckhardt (1818–1897), a Swiss scholar of classical antiquity and the Renaissance, said that the end of classical Greece and the advent of the Hellenistic age coincided with the objective decline of the polis, which was by this point incapable of producing genuine political personalities. A changing of the guard was at hand with the advent of Alexander III of Macedon. For that matter, Skepticism, Epicureanism, and Stoicism, three of the leading schools of Hellenistic philosophy, were already perhaps a reaction to the progressive disintegration of the ancient world and the decline of the polis.

The formation of the Hellenistic kingdoms following the death of Alexander III (the Great) brought with it a profound cultural transformation that saw Greek culture spread throughout the Mediterranean but also merge with various other traditions, and in the process lose its original unique qualities. In a situation where the Greeks were losing the political liberty and independence of the *poleis*, those three schools presented a similar objective, though one that was to be attained in different ways. They also offered a set of theoretical and practical values that depended on an individual's conscience while also guaranteeing coexistence and allowing the integration into increasingly complex political systems of the great new structures of state and, later, empire that were eventually to supplant the city-state.

According to an apothegm of Plutarch, Philip II of Macedon, upon being told that a certain city he wished to conquer was impregnable, replied to his advisers, "Is there not a pathway to it wide enough for an ass laden with gold?"[12] The father of Alexander the Great was hardly being ironic. Philip II had managed to wrest from Athenian control the gold and silver mines of Thracia, and he made much better use of them than anyone had before. All the same, when Alexander the Great came to power, in 336 B.C., he discovered that he was short of cash—in fact, this was one of the main factors driving his effort to expand the boundaries of his empire, even though the great general never managed to accumulate and set aside the treasures of the nations he conquered, since that gold was immediately put back into circulation in order to pay his troops and finance the needs of his new empire.

Was Alexander a great statesman? That's not all he was, according to what we read in Saint Augustine's *City of God* concerning the pirate captured by Alexander: "Indeed, that was an apt and true reply which was given to Alexander the Great by a pirate who had been seized. For when that king asked the man what he meant by keeping hostile possession of the sea, he answered with bold pride, 'What thou meanest by seizing the whole earth; but because I do it with a petty ship, I am called a robber, whilst thou who dost it with a great fleet art styled emperor.' "[13] (The anecdote was also cited by Cicero in his *De Republica*.)

And, comparable with the concept of bullying abuse, if the notion of corruption is also a question of scale, the transition from city-state to empire cannot have but held very unpleasant surprises for the future.

THREE BRIBES IN ANCIENT ROME

From Verres to Tacitus

THE ACRONYM R.O.M.A.—standing for *radix omnium malorum avaritia*, "Greed is the root of all evil"—probably dates from the fourth century A.D., but in the political life of ancient Rome, corruption had already taken on quite a considerable scale before then. Yet the structures of the Roman state stood solid for many centuries before being gravely undermined. Notoriously, the great Julius Caesar (100–44 B.C.) made use of all and any means—not merely violence but also financial means—to attain the consulate, dismiss the corrupt Senate, and become the founder of a new Rome. Plutarch writes,

> When Metellus, the tribune, would have hindered [Caesar] from taking money out of the public treasure, and adduced some laws against it, Caesar replied, that

arms and laws had each their own time; "If what I do
displeases you, leave the place; war allows no free talking. When I have laid down my arms, and made peace,
come back and make what speeches you please. And
this," he added, "I will tell you in diminution of my
own just right, as indeed you and all others who have
appeared against me and are now in my power, may
be treated as I please." Having said this to Metellus, he
went to the doors of the treasury, and the keys being
not to be found, sent for smiths to force them open.[1]

And he thus took possession of 15,000 gold ingots,
30,000 silver ingots, and 30 million sesterces. In order to
secure his election, he contracted a number of debts and
financed his own campaign by dipping with both hands
into the tubs of cash made available to him by individuals such as Crassus, a wealthy building contractor who
was later paid back with public works contracts. In fact,
it was Caesar, along with Crassus and Pompey, who first
introduced the custom of corrupting the public at a steep
cost.

There were certainly plenty of voices raised against
them. The Roman historian Sallust (86–35 B.C.) described
and sternly condemned the most licentious customs of
Rome and her rulers. "For the nobles used their high rank
and the common folk their liberty as a means to the grati-
fication of their desires, and each man appropriated or
laid violent hands on whatever took his fancy," we read
in Sallust's *Historiae*:

So society was divided into two parties, and the body
of the state in which they had been united was rent

asunder. The nobles, however, had the advantage in party strife, while the power of the people was of less effect, being distributed and dissolved among so many. The will of a few men determined both military and domestic policy: the treasury, provinces, and magistracies, the glories and triumphs of war were all in these men's hands, while the people suffered the hardships of poverty and military service. The spoils of war were seized by the generals and a chosen few; meanwhile the parents and babes of the soldiers were driven from their homes by powerful neighbours.[2]

Seeking, as was his wont, the cause of events in the vices or virtues of individuals, Sallust also delved into the conspiracy of Catiline (108–62 B.C.), concluding that the leaders of the parties then in power were to be held responsible for the "profanation" of public life.

This must have been a world that Sallust knew very well, given the fact that he held an office of some importance in the province and he left a very bad memory (at least in these terms) of himself. He exploited a wealthy land to the last drop with bribery and heavy taxation, and he did it to such an extent that he scandalized even his contemporaries, who were of course quite jaded to such customs. When put on trial, Sallust was obliged to turn to Caesar for protection. Caesar did intervene with the judges on behalf of his friend, to such an extent that the court acquitted him. The money that he had extorted was used in part to build a villa for Caesar near Tivoli and in part to plant and build splendid gardens around his own Roman villa.

Jérôme Carcopino (1881–1970), a French historian of Rome, claims that Catiline's conspiracy does not occupy as prominent a place in history as Cicero's *Catilinarian Orations* occupy in literature. Other scholars disagree, and have seen Catiline as the inventor of the coup d'état, a romantic idealist revolutionary and in any case an individual with great ambitions, pitted in a struggle against the oligarchy of the Roman Senate. Let us even admit that he is not as important as Sallust or Cicero (and that a good deal of the light that illuminates those two historians actually does not come from Catiline at all), it is still not clear why we should deny him his place in history. Even if it were only to recall the charges of malfeasance, Catiline's promises of a general cancellation of debt in case of electoral victory, and the great contradictions that every self-proclaimed idealist inevitably carries with him.

Verres (120–43 B.C.), governor of Sicily and propraetor in that province from 73 to 70 B.C., became in a certain sense the original archetype of the callous "bribe-o-crat": it is calculated that he stole from the Roman tax rolls more than 40 million sesterces (a legionary at the time earned around 900 sesterces a year) and looted the province with scientific and methodical determination, and this certainly should have been enough to make him stand out as an exception. Yet even Cicero, his accuser, who had every imaginable interest in presenting him as an exemplary case of greed taking power, said that his conduct only represented the norm in much of the Roman empire.

The absence of a proper bureaucratic apparatus inevitably resulted in the delegation of numerous administrative functions, from collecting taxes to issuing contracts for the construction of public works. It was therefore understood that magistrates would get rich during their terms in office. In Verres's case, when his defense was handled by the renowned Roman orator Quintus Hortensius Hortalus, it is said that the bribes offered to the jurors were insufficient to win his acquittal. The evidence gathered by Cicero was overwhelming, and before the verdict could be returned, Verres escaped into exile in Marseilles, where he lived surrounded by the artworks he'd made away with—at least until his execution, on Mark Antony's orders.

But Cicero's fortunes began to decline with the case of the patrician Publius Clodius Pulcher, the protagonist of a great scandal in 62 B.C. when, dressed as a woman, Clodius entered the house of Julius Caesar during the celebration of the mysteries of the vestal virgins and brought disgrace on Caesar's wife. Cicero brought charges of sacrilege, but Clodius, probably as a result of an extensive campaign of corruption, won the case. The result was that Caesar divorced his wife and Clodius earned the undying hatred of Cicero, who was sent into exile.

The historian Tacitus (A.D. 58–117), a senator and austere proponent of republican morality, was an adversary of despotism and was hostile to the corruption of imperial power. "Even in Rome, . . ." he wrote in lapidary style, "all things hideous and shameful from every part of the world find their centre and become popular."[3] In A.D. 100, accompanied by Pliny the Younger, Tacitus stood as an accuser in the trial for misappropriation against the proconsul of Africa, Marius Priscus, but in reality, the founder of "modern" history, who made the relationship between ethics and power one of the fundamental themes of his work, began his political career thanks to the influence of the general Julius Agricola, whose fourteen-year-old daughter Tacitus married in A.D. 77.

Tacitus himself, in the preface to *The Histories*, provides us with some information about his career path: "My elevation was begun by Vespasian, augmented by Titus, and still further advanced by Domitian." He was *tribunus militum* (military tribune) around 76, quaestor in 81–82, and praetor in 86. That same year he was elected to the priestly college of the *quindecemviri sacris faciundis* (literally, "a college of fifteen men to perform sacred actions"), which certainly indicates the respect that Tacitus enjoyed in the Senate and among the populace. After his time as a praetor, in any case, he lived through a difficult period until he reached the consulate in 97. At that point, finally enjoying a certain financial tranquility, he began to write his masterpieces, while continuing with his public activity.

We should devote a chapter all its own to what we could refer to as the "military sphere" in Rome. Military commanders were not subject to any punishment whatsoever if they enriched themselves with the plunder of war, which was actually considered the legitimate possession of the victorious general. Certainly, war booty was less corruption, strictly speaking, than perhaps a "legitimate percentage" on the business at hand, a custom that certainly constituted not only a way of paying the armies but also an exceptional incentive to Roman expansionism. Foreign policy, it was clear, was not only a matter of centurions and triremes. In international relations as well, money held an absolutely privileged position.

Foreign gold was always a great temptation and a natural justification when it was a matter of exporting the Pax Romana to the rest of the world. There is no shortage of examples: the rivalry between the Numidians Adherbal and Jugurtha on the death of Massinissa (148 B.C.) was settled by the cunning and "generosity" of the latter. Rome had initially subscribed to the cause of Adherbal, who had sent ambassadors to the city, but Jugurtha's gold soon induced the senators to change their minds. "And so," Sallust writes,

> he too shortly sent ambassadors to Rome, laden with silver and gold, and charged first to glut his old friends with gifts, then to win new friends and to effect all that lay within the power of bribes to perform. When the ambassadors were come to Rome, . . . they sent splendid gifts to his friends and others who at that time were powerful in the senate, whereby they so changed men's opinion that Jugurtha's cause, for which the nobles had shown little liking, now became very dear to them.[4]

Now it is true that this was not enough to prevent a war against Massinissa's adoptive son, but in that case, too, Jugurtha's proverbial "generosity" was sufficient to ensure that he went largely unpunished. But when Jugurtha finally reached Rome to defend himself against the "defamatory charges" that had been brought by the Senate, he was forced to turn and flee again for his life. "The story runs that on his departure he kept looking back at Rome with never a word. At last he broke silence and said, 'A city for sale and ripe for ruin if once she can find a purchaser!'"[5]

Another exemplary case took place in 187 B.C., we are told by the historian of Rome, Titus Livius, known as

Livy (59 B.C.–A.D. 17). Lucius Scipio Asiaticus, brother
of Scipio Africanus, was accused of having negotiated a
peace treaty for money with the Syrian king Antiochus:

> In order to secure more favourable terms of peace for
> Antiochus, Scipio had received six thousand pounds
> of gold, and four hundred and eighty pounds of sil-
> ver. . . . There is a tradition that an accounting for just
> this sum was also demanded in the Senate from Pub-
> lius Scipio himself, and that, when he had directed his
> brother Lucius to bring the account-book, he had
> himself, with his own hands, torn it up, being angry
> that after he had brought two hundred millions into
> the treasury he should be asked to account for four
> millions.[6]

"Vice that is powerless is called virtue," observed
the philosopher Seneca (4 B.C.–A.D. 65), with a turn of
phrase that is reminiscent of the wordplay of certain
seventeenth-century moralists.[7] Originally from Cordoba
and an admirer of Cicero, Seneca distinguished himself
not only for being a master rhetorician but also for his
involvement in a number of episodes of corruption and
conspiracy. Although he paid lip service to a defense of
the interests of the plebs, there are those who consider
him to have been the intellectual in service to power par
excellence, a figure of particularly dubious morality if we
admit that corruption of the intelligence, as the philosopher-
emperor Marcus Aurelius maintained, is more dangerous
than environmental corruption.

In his *Epistulae morales ad Lucilium*, Seneca himself
dwells on the question, and although he confesses no

guilt, he does seem to reflect on his own conduct as well: "No era in history has ever been free from blame. Moreover, if you once begin to take account of the irregularities belonging to any particular era, you will find—to man's shame be it spoken—that sin never stalked abroad more openly than in Cato's very presence." He goes on:

> I say that all men hide their sins and, even though the issue be successful, enjoy the results while concealing the sins themselves. A good conscience, however, wishes to come forth and be seen of men; wickedness fears the very shadows. . . . It had gone ill with us, owing to the many crimes which escape the vengeance of the law and the prescribed punishments, were it not that those grievous offences against nature must pay the penalty in ready money, and that in place of suffering the punishment comes fear.[8]

The regularly recurring appointment at the voting urn has long been one of the most favorable opportunities to put into practice the tradition of bribery and the market for favor swapping. In ancient Rome, according to the poet Horace (65–8 B.C.), a candidate for a magistrature used to go to visit his voters usually accompanied by a fair number of supporters and parasites, as well as some influential celebrity capable of bringing as many votes to him as possible. The candidate, moreover, usually shook hands with all the voters, familiarly greeting them by name with the assistance of a quick-witted prompter.

The consul Murena was accused of having paid the crowd of his entourage during the electoral campaign, but Cicero defended him brilliantly, successfully elevating the traditional role played by the humble category of electoral supporters:

> Do not, then, O Cato, deprive the lower class of men of this power of showing their dutiful feelings; allow these men, who hope for everything from us, to have something also themselves, which they may be able to give us. If they have nothing beyond their own vote, that is but little; since they have no interest which they can exert in the votes of others. They themselves, as they are accustomed to say, cannot plead for us, cannot go bail for us, cannot invite us to their houses; but they ask all these things of us, and do not think that they can requite the services which they receive from us by anything but by their attentions of this sort.[9]

The organization of a campaign banquet was a crucial moment in the promotion of a candidate. Quintus Cicero points it out insistently to his brother Marcus Tullius in his *Handbook on Canvassing for the Consulship*: "Liberality is, again, of wide application; it is shewn in regard to the management of your private property. . . . It may also be displayed in banquets, which you must take care to attend yourself and to cause your friends to attend, whether open ones or those confined to particular tribes."[10] Again, in his oration *Pro Murena*, Cicero declares that he is entirely in agreement with his brother senator:

> But I must change my tone for Cato argues with me on rigid and stoic principles. He says that it is not true that good-will is conciliated by food. He says that men's judgments, in the important business of electing

to magistracies, ought not to be corrupted by pleasures. Therefore, if any one, to promote his canvass, invites another to supper, he must be condemned. 'Shall you,' says he, 'seek to obtain supreme power, supreme authority, and the helm of the republic, by encouraging men's sensual appetites, by soothing their minds, by tendering luxuries to them? Are you asking employment as a pimp from a band of luxurious youths, or the sovereignty of the world from the Roman people?' An extraordinary sort of speech! but our usages, our way of living, our manners, and the constitution itself rejects it. For the Lacedaemonians, the original authors of that way of living and of that sort of language, men who lie at their daily meals on hard oak benches, and the Cretans, of whom no one ever lies down to eat at all, have neither of them preserved their political constitutions or their power better than the Romans, who set apart times for pleasure as well as times for labour.[11]

FOUR THE FECES OF THE DEVIL

Social and Ecclesiastical Corruption between Feudalism and Rise of the Merchants

ACCORDING TO JOHN NOONAN, the author of *Bribes*, the genuine era of corruption, understood as reciprocity and the exchange of favors in order to carry on relations with one's neighbors or the powerful, ended with the spread of Christian morality and, in particular, with the centuries that came on the heels of the end of the Roman empire: the "age of the barbarians" and the Early Middle Ages (fifth to tenth century). And yet the mechanism of reciprocity continued to serve as a glue for social relations later as well. Think of the exchange between rights and protection and the culture of submission in exchange for peaceful living that underlies the relationship of vassalage between subjects and lords, and therefore the feudal system as a whole, a system that, in the Middle Ages, and for hundreds of years, was destined to characterize the organization of social relations and power in the Old World. As a political formula it had already been established in late imperial Roman society, and it sank its roots deep into the prior custom of *clientes* (patronage and protection).

An unmistakable confusion between public law and private law characterizes the entire Middle Ages, an era in which landowners felt they had been invested with sovereign rights over those who lived on their property. Moreover, the confusion between local and central power and the clash, if not the intermingling, of secular power and religious power favored the spread of an extensive social corruption. "Born in the midst of a very loosely-knit society, in which commerce was insignificant and money a rarity," the French historian Marc Bloch observes in his book, *Feudal Society*, "European feudalism underwent a fundamental change as soon as the meshes of the human network had been drawn closer together and the circulation of goods and coin intensified."[1] But above and beyond all social and political transformations, over the entire arc of medieval history, the conflict between the ideal of purity in Christian morality and the reality of power wielding was more than a simple passing phenomenon. It would ultimately have lasting consequences over the centuries as embodied in corruption and the practice of bribe taking and giving.

Saint Augustine (A.D. 354–430)—who had a great deal to do with courts of law for much of his life, first as a judge in Hippo, in modern-day Algeria, and later as a plaintiff in Ravenna—expands the array of cases in his reflections on the topic, considering the possible corruption of judge and functionary, not merely in terms of the "classic" *munera* (gold and silver) but also the so-called "presents of hospitality," offerings, and even praise and adulation toward those who make decisions from a position of authority. His was an extremely strict view, considering the customs of the church of that time. In fact, how could the church even survive without *munera*? By this point in the fourth century, especially in some areas in the East, it had become customary for bishops to demand the payment of sums of money from those who were ordained to new ecclesiastical positions. It was a form, so to speak, of royalty on divine grace and another piece in the more widespread puzzle of marketing that, with the sale of indulgences and other simoniac practices, acquired over time a spread and a scale that were truly worrisome. The Fourth Ecumenical Council, in Chalcedon in A.D. 451, expressly condemned the sale of ecclesiastical positions, and in 790 Charlemagne, too, condemned whosoever accepted gifts and offerings as staining themselves with the "heresy of Simon Magus." Still, after a thousand years of Christianity, that heresy had become the rule. Religious institution were largely exploited for personal benefits, and the urgent need for reform was becoming more evident with every passing day.

Pope Boniface VIII, who in 1300 in Rome proclaimed the first Christian Jubilee (a year of forgiveness and remissions of sins), was one of the popes who with the greatest force and conviction attempted to impose the church's temporal power, and considered Vatican business basically to be a family affair, to the point that Dante placed him in Hell, planted in the ground with the flat of his feet aflame. Montaigne (1533–1592) would write, "Boniface VIII, they say, entered office like a fox, behaved in it like a lion, and died like a dog."[2] Dante is without a doubt among the men who best summarize the spirit of his time where the perception of corruption is concerned. In *De Monarchia* he makes reference, and it is surely no accident, to a dualism similar "to the horizon which lies between the two hemispheres. . . . He alone of all beings partakes of the perishable and the imperishable." Perhaps this explains the "twofold end" of man, divided between the happiness of this life on earth and an ambition to achieve eternal life.[3]

In the circles of Hell described by Dante in the *Divine Comedy*, we find the seven deadly sins of Christian morality (sloth, greed, gluttony, envy, wrath, lust, and pride), to which are added the "lesser" sins such as cowardice, fraud, idolatry, inconstancy, infidelity, injustice, and so on.

During his descent into the Inferno, accompanied by Virgil, Dante reaches the eighth circle, where the fraudulent sinners are punished. Fraud is for Dante the vice most typical of man, the sin that most boldly defies the love and universal justice of God. The sinners punished in the fifth *bolgia* (pit) of the eighth circle of Hell are characterized in the celebrated verses of the twenty-first canto: "All there are barrators, except Bonturo [a politician in Lucca]; No into Yes for money there is changed."[4] According to Dante, in Lucca, cash can turn a no into a yes. And a public official who, for cash, agrees to turn his no into a yes is in fact a barrator. Bonturo's crime is malfeasance, the acceptance of bribery (he was, however, publicly acquitted on charges of barratry). In Dante's account, like the fraudulent, barrators are immersed in a stream of black pitch, which takes them back to the darkness of their murky business and soils them indelibly, marking them out forever for public contempt. The diabolic guardians at their heels pierce them violently with their razor-sharp talons, and tear the sinners to shreds.

But Dante's infernal imaginary world does nothing to conceal the fact that he himself, while serving as prior in Florence (a prior was a member of the city's governing body, the Signoria), was accused of bribe taking. The story, in its broad outlines, runs like this: In the summer of 1300, the Tuscan capital—its independence threatened by Pope Boniface VIII—put three papal bankers on trial in absentia. And in spite of the pontiff's objections, the six Florentine priors (Dante was a member of the moderate Guelph faction) ratified their negative judgment of the friends of Boniface. When the pope seized control of the city the following year, thanks to his alliance with Charles of Valois, Dante, along with his fellow members of government, was found guilty of having taken money in exchange for the election of the new priors, of having accepted illicit commissions for the issuance of orders and licenses to functionaries of the city government, and for having drawn from the treasury of Florence more than he should have by right. None of the defendants appeared to offer a defense, and Dante was no exception; the new podestà (an official who enforces imperial rights) issued a verdict and sentence, in absentia, that could not be appealed. If any of the guilty were to set foot on Florentine soil, they would be burned at the stake. Thus it was that Dante, at the age of thirty-seven, set off into exile.

Geoffrey Chaucer, the greatest English writer of the fourteenth century, also explores in his *Canterbury Tales* the subject of the fraudulent practices of barrators. When he speaks of barratry he refers principally to cases of extortion and simony. In one of the first tales, told by Brother Hubert, a "summoner" threatens a poor widow with excommunication unless she can pay him twelve pennies. But the man does not actually possess any power to excommunicate and for that very reason winds up condemned to hell, with a parting gift of the woman's heartfelt curse. Brother Hubert's traveling companion then goes on to tell the story of Friar John, a tireless preacher:

> "Trentals," he declared, "from penance bring
> 　　delivery
> for dead friends' souls, the old as well as young,
> All thirty masses being quickly sung—
> Not meaning in a frivolous kind of way,
> Although a priest would sing but one a day.
> Get out their souls, deliver them," he'd call,
> "For hard it is by meathook and by awl
> To get a clawing, or to burn and bake.
> Make haste, get going at it, for Christ's sake!"[5]

The episodes of simony described by Chaucer are many and varied. One of the characters most vividly described is that of the seller of indulgences, who has come directly from Rome to visit the reliquary of Thomas Becket. His bag is full of indulgences, "piping hot, newly arrived from Rome." And that's not all: he also brings with him an assortment of absolutely extraordinary relics, ranging from a pillowcase, which he presents as part of the Virgin Mary's veil, to a corner of cloth that he assures was a tiny strip of the sail of Saint Peter's fishing boat.

Needless to say, the men and women harangued by the merchant of grace and indulgence mostly give in to his deceit and prove to be proud and pleased to honor the relics of the saints, convinced as they are that they're redeeming themselves from their sins and ingratiating themselves with the Lord. There are only a few who really rebel against the practice of simony, and the reason is unmistakable: being able to pay cash on the barrelhead for the absolution of one's sins is a bargain for everyone, both rich and poor.

Only later Martin Luther forcefully attacked that ecclesiastical custom when he nailed up his Ninety-five Theses on the door of the Wittenberg Castle Church: "Christians are to be taught that if the pope knew the exactions of the pardon-preachers, he would rather that Saint Peter's church should go to ashes, than that it should be built up with the skin, flesh and bones of his sheep"; "The treasures of the indulgences are nets with which they now fish for the riches of men."[6]

If Marco Polo (1254–1324) was the incarnation of the entrepreneurial and business spirit of the fourteenth century, it should be noted that in 1283 in London there was already a Lombard Street where fourteen Italian banks were in operation, and in Paris just a few years later there were already more than twenty Italian "credit institutes." A tradition of family and business recollections has taken root, the Italian literary critic and philologian Vittore Branca points out in an anthology he edited as a sort of full-fledged collective composition illuminating the significance that in that period was assigned to earning and profit, ownership of home and property, and, broadening the point of view, the conception of the individual, his role in society, the meaning of the state and, in the background, the perception of death and the afterlife. Bourgeois and merchants—who between the Middle Ages and the Renaissance represent the great new social development, according to Branca has—provided a practical and everyday counterpoint to the reflections of the philosophers and the compositions of the men of letters who were living every day, in the choices of their profession, the contradictions of an era caught between the desire to save one's soul and the compromises necessary for success. Most of those *mercatanti* lived in the last days of the era of free communes, as city governments were called, and were part, whether in victory or defeat, of the rise of the already all-powerful Medici family and were largely bound up with its economic good fortune. "It is a very fine and grand thing to know how to earn money, but an even finer and greater thing is to know how to spend it properly and in a measured manner," wrote the Florentine merchant Paolo da Certaldo.[7] The common denominator of his memories, like those of Giovanni Morelli, Buonaccorso Pitti, Domenico Lenzi, Donato Velluti, Lapo Piccolini (an important member of the powerful Arte della Lana, the wool guild), or again of Bernardo Machiavelli and Francesco Datini (a man of Prato who declared that he possessed over 1,500 florins in the currency of the time), is the hunt for money and wealth, to the verge of audacity, the daring exploitation of capital, the increasingly inextricable intertwining between public and private sphere, the ambition to attain public office, the prevalence of market and family considerations over all else. Even if a certain moralistic and slightly self-righteous twist characterizes this massive autobiographical effort ("in the name of God and money"), it is justified by the fact that, as again Paolo da Certaldo writes, it is always good "not to manifest your secrets to a person of whom you are not entirely certain."[8]

Boccaccio's *Decameron* in this sense offers a perfect portrait gallery of the Italian "pre-bourgeoisie" of the time: cunning, swindling merchants such as Ser Ciappelletto, or merchants swindled by one and all such as Andreuccio from Perugia, as well as bored aristocrats, foolish peasants, and so on (Boccaccio himself was the son of a functionary of the Bardi, and there are scholars who have identified in his metaphors the same language used by the businessmen of the era).

As shown by Yves Renouard, as early as the tenth century Venice and Amalfi were trading with the East, and it was in that period that the first individuals identifiable as "businessmen" appeared. Two such figures are Mauro and Pantaleone of Amalfi. Starting in the twelfth century, however, that trade became the monopoly of the Italian maritime republics, and Renouard himself describes Genoa as a "hotbed of individualism"—he had in mind especially characters such as the profiteer Benedetto Zaccaria. In Florence and Venice there was a general flourishing of banks, fixed-interest loans, and letters of credit, and the techniques of business would go on developing until they culminated in the fourteenth century in the creation of such financial instruments as the promissory note, double-entry bookkeeping, checking accounts, checkbooks, and the earliest forms of insurance. "Within the framework of medieval unity," writes the historian Giuseppe Galasso, "in eleventh- and twelfth-century Italy the great flourishing of the communes took place," a municipal development that would lead to an Italy "in which the merchant's counter would take the place of weapons as a status symbol and a path to social elevation; an Italy in which gold has value as a tool for the creation of new wealth."[9]

And little would change in reality with the *signorie*, or seigniories, which, "far from being a free and direct expression" of the people's will, inevitably constituted "an aristocracy composed first and foremost of major businessmen." Among the earliest capitalists were the Florentine bankers, who lent money to kings and aristocrats who had to maintain armies and fight wars against each other, on various fronts and with a diverse array of pretexts. The Ricciardi family of Lucca financed Edward I and his conquest of Wales; the Frescobaldis of Florence underwrote the war that Edward II waged against Scotland; the Bardis and the Peruzzis of Florence allowed Edward III to start the Hundred Years' War against France (and as collateral or assurance of the return of the loan, what was often at stake were the crown's own holdings), receiving in exchange—at the very least—great political influence. Not that there was anything new about bankers making loans at interest: usury was already widespread in ancient times. Solon speaks of it as early as the second half of the seventh century B.C., even though among the first Israelites, as well as for many other peoples, to ask interest on a loan was condemned on moral grounds, if not outright forbidden, and the same was later the case among the Christians.

The conflicted response to the charging of interest is evident in the role played by merchants and bankers who lent money to cities and princes, and even more powerful rulers. This conflict is relevant to understanding the centrality of usury to the West's economic system for eight centuries, from the twelfth to the nineteenth; this is clearly reconstructed by Jacques Le Goff in *Your Money or Your Life: Economy and Religion in the Middle Ages*. He describes the conflicts around the charging of interest as an explosive blend of economics and religion, money and salvation: "The medieval usurer found himself in a strange situation. Within a history of the *longue durée* (. . . the deeply rooted and slowly changing), the usurer is the precursor of capitalism, an economic system that, despite its injustices and failings, is part of the West's trajectory of progress." And in that sense, "Although not committing a sin according to either the Jewish law or the Christian one, the Jewish usurer, increasingly driven to usury by Christian society, was experiencing a period of increasing anti-Semitism, based upon latent anti-Jewishness fanned by the struggle against usury undertaken by the Church and by the Christian princes."[10]

A moralizing standpoint, that of the church, did not always rest on unassailable moral foundations. In fact, over the centuries of mercantile and commercial development the decadence of the papal court continued unarrested, and may perhaps have reached its apex in the time of Pope Alexander VI, Rodrigo Borgia. Georg Burckhardt, better known by his pseudonym, George Spalatin, the chaplain and secretary in the court of Frederick III the Wise, Elector of Saxony, records in his diary that in 1501 fifty courtesans dined at the apostolic palace and, after the meal was done, danced naked before the pontiff. Rodrigo Borgia's election to the papal throne on August 11, 1492, was nothing less than the culmination of a career path built with boldness and shamelessness. At the time he had seven children four of whom were born to him by his "official" mistress, and three by other women. It was with Alexander VI that the sales of indulgences and ecclesiastical offices enjoyed such unabashed proliferation that it was deemed scandalous even in a society apparently willing to turn a blind eye to the most nefarious deeds. An office especially for the purpose of selling indulgences, the Dataria, had been established and tasked with putting that business into some semblance of order. Pope Alexander VI was able to draw directly on the funds of the Datarìa to satisfy his need for cash to further his own personal ambition and those of his children, in particular those of Cesare Borgia, the Valentino, who was determined to create a powerful state in central Italy. The friar Girolamo Savonarola, well known for his apocalyptic antipapal preaching, who was tried for heresy and burned at the stake, was fond of saying in reference to the Roman Catholic Church that whoever had the money should hurry to Rome, where everything was for sale. But alongside the literature of the era that makes reference to similar episodes and the general undertow of corruption, there were also such singular cases of silence as that of the Dominican theologian Thomas Aquinas (1225–1275). Although he was well aware of the customs of the papal court, he never made any explicit reference to the problem of corruption that prevailed there.

The measures adopted by a number of pontiffs— specific sanctions, the foundation of religious orders, the resumption of theological teachings—were not enough to halt the spreading corruption. Thus, the Protestant Reformation and its success was a natural response to the decadence of the Roman Catholic Church.

Above and beyond the condemnation of corruption, the Reformation led to a break with the predominant Catholic culture and the birth of a Protestant ethic that would, however, establish an objective correlation between worldly economic success and salvation in the afterlife. It is no accident that the German economist and sociologist Max Weber (1864–1920), who wrote major works on ethics in politics, would view this religious revolution as the foundation of the flourishing of commerce that we saw develop, the early rise of capitalism, and in a certain sense the subsequent development of the bourgeoisie. According to Weber's analysis, economic success in the context of the rise of Protestantism and, more particularly, Calvinism began to be seen as a manifestation of divine grace. This in spite of the fact that businessmen—by turns merchants, artisans, entrepreneurs, fixers, and captains of industry— were not always figures of sterling rectitude. Almost two centuries before Luther's theses shook the church, the Tuscan poet Petrarch (1304–1374), Francesco Petrarca, had written in one of his epistles: "We, dear friend, now have everything made of gold—lances and shields and chains and coronets; . . . Gold enslaves the free and frees the slaves; it acquits evil-doers. . . . by making the noble-hearted, the powerful, the learned, the handsome, and—it may surprise you to hear it—even the saintly its masters."[11]

Two centuries after Petrarch, in 1532, a man from Florence would analyze a ruler's duties and the relations between secular and religious power in a lucid work we still read today: Machiavelli's *The Prince*.

FIVE CORRUPTION IN POWER

From Machiavelli to the Gold of the New World

THE PRINCE by Machiavelli is a crucial text in the history of corruption, both in terms of its interpretation of the past and for the understanding it provides of the era in which it was composed and the long period of influence it can still claim. Of the prince Machiavelli wrote, "And yet he must not mind incurring the disgrace of those vices without which it would be difficult to save the state, for if one considers well, it will be found that some things which seem virtues would, if followed, lead to one's ruin, and some others which appear vices result, if followed, in one's greater security and wellbeing."[1] According to Giuseppe Prezzolini (1882–1982), an Italian writer, publisher, and literary critic who had witnessed the Great War and did not look kindly on his country's idle and corrupted ruling class, Machiavelli "discovered that evil is inherent in all political action aimed at the common good. He contrasted the ideal portraits of statesmen possessed of angelic purity and superior skills with the harsh and regrettable reality of a political leader willing to commit the sins of humanity in order to increase humanity's welfare, and with no fear of treading the paths of evils."[2] Francesco Guicciardini (1483–1540), a political historian, adviser to the Medici, and a friend and critic of Machiavelli's, belonged to the same school of thought as Machiavelli. To him, political action always appeared to be triggered by some self-interested impulse; it is a way of pursuing opportunity and it never halts in the face of despicable deeds, if they are required to attain success. His is a wisdom that comes very close to corruption. He confesses that he was guilty of having tended to his own "private" good, but he finds a justification in the general human condition and in the specific nature of the times in which he lived. The writer Indro Montanelli (1909–2001) seemed to have no doubts about this matter: "Guicciardini is the true teacher of the Italians. A monster of selfishness and opportunism who never even bothered to pretend to be otherwise."[3]

The historian Giuseppe Galasso described the political scene of the Renaissance as follows: "Politics is strength and cunning; all moral aspiration is excluded; only the naïve would try to introduce it. Those who engage in politics and revolve in the orbit of power, at whatever level, perform an activity that translates into commandeering, bullying, or opportunities for illicit good fortune." This was "a form of politics that had more to do with the strength of gold than the might of steel," writes the historian Gioacchino Volpe (1876–1971).[4]

We may wonder whether the Burckhardtian concept of individualism is valid, especially when applied to a period as complex and ever-changing as the period from the end of the Middle Ages to the sixteenth century, but in any case it is overused and somewhat simplistic. It is therefore all the more necessary to underscore the point that Machiavelli's political theory is actually based on his insight regarding an opposition between civil coexistence and political action on the one hand and corruption on the other. In Machiavelli's eyes corruption meant a lack of virtue. By this idea of opposition Machiavelli meant that the civil coexistence and political action always rule out corruption. The recurrent theme in his writings is the search for political and moral institutional remedies to prevent and uproot political corruption. The figure of the moralist that begins to appear with Machiavelli and Guicciardini, wrote the critic Giovanni Macchia,

> is certainly a killer of myths. There lies his courage and his reason for existence. A moralist does not apply himself to the construction of a way of thought: he limits himself to noticing the contradictory nature of life. . . . Let us abandon those dreamers of a 'perfect society,' the utopianists, the dreary optimists, [who] are often the very worst moralists of all and who fail to live up to the vision of the concrete man, out of idealistic zeal or cowardice.[5]

A corrupt friar is one of the most clearly drawn characters in Machiavelli's comedy *Mandragola* (The Mandrake), and it is surely no accident, since it is also a concrete demonstration of the author's fundamental political theorem. At the high point of the play, the parasite Ligurio, in the service of young Callimaco, enlists the help of Friar Timoteo to convince the faithful and modest Lucrezia, married to Messer Nicia, that it is necessary for her to yield to "higher considerations": she must sleep one night with a stranger in order to be healed of her infertility and save her marriage. In Timoteo's words we see the primacy of ends over means (not to mention the primacy of monetary considerations over moral ones, as the friar's services are by no means cheap): "As far as your conscience is concerned, you have these general premises: where there is a certain good and an evil that is uncertain, you should never abandon the good for fear of the evil."[6]

One of the most noteworthy voices of the Renaissance is Baldassarre Castiglione (1478–1529), who served in the court of the Montefeltro family in Urbino and as a diplomat and papal nuncio at the court of Emperor Charles V of Spain. The authentic greatness of his major work, *The Courtier*, lies in the fact that the social life whose conventions are so gracefully described by the author is based on falsehood and deceit, and quite rightly so, because to truly speak one's mind at any time can only lead to struggle and bitterness—particularly dangerous among the world's rulers.

Everyone knows that without hypocrisy human relations would not be possible, hence the necessity of a codex of premeditated dissimulations. Castiglione knew very well the ways of his world, since he was as comfortable with weapons as with words, as familiar with the dangers of a battlefield as with the traps of a court. Only with a high degree of dissimulation could one survive relations among rulers, diatribes among courtiers, the moral decay of the great houses, and the sins and peccadilloes of the papal court. This type of dissimulation was not to be considered corruption, but mere coexistence.

We can apply the same lens in our reading of the *Galateo* by Monsignor Giovanni Della Casa (1503–1556), a man of letters and the secretary of state under Pope Paul IV. Della Casa, even as he laid out a utopian model of the reconciliation of public and private affairs, has become known as the herald of form over substance. But form, in his view, *is* substance, and the refinements of the art of living in society are what keeps society together. He emphasized that alongside the need for good manners, "Justice, fortitude, and the other greater and nobler virtues are called into service more infrequently."[7] Also, he added, because "men hate their same vices when glimpsed in other men." More explicit in this sense would be *Proxeneta, seu de prudentia civili* (The mediator, or civic prudence), a learned handbook of politics written just after 1550 by the philosopher, scientist, and mathematician Girolamo Cardano (1501–1576). This treatise discusses the figure of the mediator—a diplomatic, middleman, or fixer—and Cardano was explicit in putting his readers explicitly on guard against the dissolute and profit-seeking nature of such individuals. He also sought to put forth a number of pieces of shrewd practical advice in the realm of what we might nowadays describe as Machiavellian conduct, which no doubt reflected the nature, character, and life of the author himself. The book's thesis (not much different from the Neapolitan writer Torquato Accetto's *Della dissimulazione onesta* (On honest dissimulation), or

The Politicians' Breviary by Cardinal Jules Mazarin, is in fact that it is permissible to deceive the dishonest in a world where good and evil are never clearly separable.

The artistic symbolism of the period is indicative as seen in the works of Pieter Bruegel the Elder: *The Triumph of Death* shows a skeleton on horseback ready to strike down all those who enjoy privilege, wealth, and power. In *Dulle Griet* (known an *Mad Meg*) a man with a derriere shaped like an eggshell expels excrement, possibly gold coins, which the crowd hurries to collect. In the *Netherlandish Proverbs*, Bruegel denounces the moral and political chaos of his time by depicting a world turned upside down. In *The Land of Cockaigne* a farmer, a cleric, and a soldier represent the three layers of the society of the time—commonfolk, clergy, and nobility—all equally wrapped up in the metaphor of sin. In the works of Hieronymus Bosch we again find the theme of sin and corruption, as in his celebrated *The Seven Deadly Sins* (possibly the work of a follower), commissioned by Philip II of Spain, in which avarice is represented by a corrupt official shown taking a bribe while his free hand is outstretched for yet another.

Allegories and reality both provide confirmation of an obsession with an extraordinary moral decadence that demanded a remedy. This decadence, among other things, stimulated the flourishing throughout Europe of an extensive body of literature on the nobility that contrasted it with the new merchant classes. One such work is *Civil conversazione* (The civil conversation) by Stefano Guazzo; another is Torquato Tasso's *Gerusalemme liberata* (Jerusalem delivered), which filled the need to recall the moral and religious actions undertaken by the nobility with the Crusades in the Holy Land.

The theme of corruption is central in the work of William Shakespeare: Just think of *Measure for Measure*, or his political dramas such as *Julius Caesar*, where the English bard gives voice to both sides of the argument, the pros and cons of corruption. After the assassination of the emperor, Caesar, Brutus and Cassius argue over the under-the-table offers of the Sardians to Lucio Pella and the sale of offices, from which Cassius is determined to wring every last cent. Brutus harshly upbraids his comrade: "Remember March," he implores, "the ides of March remember: did not great Julius bleed for justice' sake? What villain touch'd his body, that did stab, and not for justice? What, shall one of us that struck the foremost man of all this world but for supporting robbers, shall we now contaminate our fingers with base bribes, and sell the mighty space of our large honours for so much trash as may be grasped thus? I had rather be a dog, and bay the moon, than such a Roman." And then think of King Lear, whose aim in distributing his wealth and land among his daughters is "that we our largest bounty may extend / Where nature doth with merit challenge," although he did fail to notice that the challenge was not between nature and merit, but between merit and interest.[8] Ben Jonson, a poet and author who was a contemporary of Shakespeare, knew the difference well when he wrote: "A heavy purse makes a light heart." His best-known and most widely translated work was *Volpone*, a story of the wealthy, parasites, and courtesans (among them the celebrated character of Mosca) that takes place in a rich, greedy, corrupt Italy, well described in the line spoken by the character Peregrine:

And he has made relation to the senate,
That you profest to him to have a plot
To sell the State of Venice to the Turk.

Around 1590 Christopher Marlowe (1564–1593) wrote *The Jew of Malta*, a play that tells the story of the drama unleashed by the decision of the governor of Malta to have the island's wealthy Jews pay the tribute exacted from the community by the Turks. One of the Jews, Barabas, who has been milked dry, plots his revenge in a crescendo of killing frenzy. The two contenders for Barabas's daughter Abigail die in a duel, and Barabas uses poison liberally to eliminate other enemies. That's not all: Once Malta falls under the siege of the Turks (which occurred in 1565), Barabas aids the foreign conquerors and thus becomes the ruler of the island. But Barabas's revenge is visited upon the Turks as well: He invites their leaders to a banquet and then hurls them down a cliff. He, too, will be betrayed and meet the same end.

The two principal themes of the play are Machiavellianism and love of money. The themes were quite characteristic of sixteenth-century England; it is no accident that the play is introduced by a character who bears the name of Machiavill and states, "I count religion but a childish toy, and hold there is no sin but ignorance."[9] Both themes are intimately connected to corruption. Much has been written about the anti-Semitism of the play, as of Shakespeare's *Merchant of Venice*, but what we want to stress here is that Barabas is the first Jew presented on the English stage in a role of any prominence. Barabas is in all likelihood Shylock's prototype, although he is far less human and pathetic than Shakespeare's character. His passion for money attains poetic flights. In his double role as a Jew and an unabashed follower of Machiavelli, whose name symbolized corruption and duplicity for all right-thinking subjects of Queen Elizabeth, Barabas was meant to offend and disturb the spectators.

All forms of public vice of the time can be found described in the *Pleasant Satyre of the Thrie Estaitis*, an allegorical drama by the Scottish poet Sir David Lyndsay, written "in commendatioun of vertew and vituperatioun of vyce." In it the three allegorized states are Spirituality (the churchmen), accompanied by Sensuality and Wantonness; Temporality (the men of government), accompanied by Public Oppression; and Merchant (businessmen). It is a satire in the spirit of Chaucer of the political, ecclesiastical, and social corruption of Scotland, which could equally apply to many of the states of Europe of the time.[10]

In the same spirit Rabelais wrote, "For among them [the Furred Law-Cats that Pantagruel meets in his adventures] vice is called virtue; wickedness, piety; treason, loyalty; robbery, justice. Plunder is their motto, and when acted by them is approved by all men, except the heretics; and all this they do because they dare; their authority is sovereign and irrefragable."[11] Generalized and widespread corruption? History tells us of Charles VIII, king of France, who as part of a wider military campaign in 1494 invaded Florence and demanded a staggering ransom to go away again. But the incorruptible Piero Capponi (1447–1496) refused to pay the ransom and tore up the paper upon which the invaders had sent their demands.

And yet history often forgets to remind us that, after negotiating on the fee and obtaining a discount of the exorbitant sum requested by the French, in the end the Florentines paid and allowed the French sovereign to continue his march down the peninsula.

In 1519, following the death of the emperor Maximilian I of Habsburg, his grandson Charles of Spain inherited the ancient dominions of the royal house of Austria and part of Burgundy, and at the same time set up his candidacy for imperial honors, relying on the enormous loans granted him by the Fuggers and the Welsers for the bribes he'd have to pay the electors of the Holy Roman Empire. Opposing his election was Francis I of France. On June 27, Charles was elected emperor by the German grand electors, in return for a promise of 850,000 florins, beating the French candidate and also overcoming the hostility of Pope Leo X. All the same, conflict immediately broke out between Emperor Charles V and France, which was by now encircled by Habsburg dominions. Francis I was captured and taken prisoner at the Battle of Pavia in 1525, and was forced to sign the onerous treaty of Madrid. (The clash between the two European powers was protracted, lasting until after the disappearance of the two initial protagonists; the Peace of Cateau-Cambrésis was signed in 1559).

In France, it was during the reign of Francis I's son, King Henry II, that the harshest persecutions began against the Huguenots. If in 1594 the head of the Protestant faction, Henry IV, was able to be crowned king of France and enter Paris, it was chiefly because the forces of the Catholic League progressively dispersed, in part as a result of the massive effort to spread corruption with which the Bourbon king purchased the acquiescence of his adversaries.

"A false document, if thought to be true for three years, can be exceedingly useful to the government." These words were written by Catherine de Medici, queen of France. She was the daughter of Lorenzo II de' Medici—himself the grandson of the more famous Lorenzo il Magnifico, to whom Machiavelli dedicated his *Prince*—and the wife of Henri, Duke of Orléans. Her portrait, crystallized by the passage of time, is that of a truly Machiavellian woman, willing to do anything in order to preserve and increase her power. Regent for her son Charles IX, she influenced the reign of Henri III and pulled no punches in her battle against the aristocratic and religious factions that were undermining the power of the crown, by ordering the notorious bloody massacre of the Huguenots on St. Bartholomew's Day, the night between August 23 and 24, 1572. Across the Channel, another woman tied her name to the English Renaissance and to the earliest dawning of what would become the British Empire: Queen Elizabeth I. We should remember that her political fortunes were in part financed by freebooters and by the predatory activities of conquest of such corsairs as Sir Francis Drake.

The journeys of discovery carried out by the great explorers of history, beginning with the discovery of the Americas by Christopher Columbus, began a conquest of virgin lands, and the exportation of the worst customs of the Old World. The hunt for fabulous wealth was increasingly the engine that drove all progress and the discovery of new worlds and brought with it inevitable abuses in the management of the new lands being subjugated and in the uses to which the revenues and resources that derived from the exploitation of those distant shores were put. Christopher Columbus wrote in a letter from Jamaica, "Gold is a Wonderful thing! Whoever possesses it is lord of all he wants. By means of gold one can even get souls into Paradise."[12] This aspiration was surely shared by the powerful who underwrote his enterprises, and was destined to lead to ruinous consequences. After the opening of the great ocean trade routes, the Portuguese, the Dutch, and the English occupied vast swathes of the Far East, South America, and Africa, inaugurating an exceptional exploitation of the native populace and a grim trade in slaves that was to go on for centuries.

Gonzalo Fernández de Oviedo y Valdés (1478–1557), a courtier in the service of the Spanish monarchy, reported in his *Historia general y natural de las Indias* that of a million natives that Columbus found on the island of Hispaniola (now Haiti) in 1535, only about 500 remained. Today, we would call it a genocide, whereas he saw it as a grace of the Lord, who had helped to eradicate from the earth's surface a people prone to sin, bestial without even the redeeming quality of animal innocence. The stereotype of the "other" to be eliminated was certainly not born here, but it did grow stronger. An opposite image of the Indios is offered by the Dominican friar Bartolomeo de las Casas (1484–1556), who almost alone opposed the looting and plunder that marked the conquest of the New World: "And of all the infinite universe of humanity, these people are the most guileless, the most devoid of wickedness and duplicity, the most obedient and faithful to their native masters and to the Spanish Christians whom they serve. . . . They are also poor people, for they not only possess little but have no desire to possess worldly goods. For this reason they are not arrogant, embittered, or greedy. . . . They are very clean in their persons, with alert, intelligent minds, docile and open to doctrine, very apt to receive our holy Catholic faith, to be endowed with virtuous customs, and to behave in a godly fashion. . . . Yet into this sheepfold, into this land of meek outcasts there came some Spaniards who immediately behaved like ravening wild beasts, wolves, tigers, or lions that had been starved for many days."[13]

In contrast to Bartolomeo, a Spanish humanist of the sixteenth century, Juan Ginés de Sepúlveda, justified the atrocities of the Spaniards by focusing on the custom of human sacrifice performed by the natives, accepted by local societies: "What temperance or mercy can you expect from men who are committed to all types of intemperance and base frivolity, and eat human flesh? And do not believe that before the arrival of the Christians they lived in the pacific kingdom of Saturn which the poets have invented; for, on the contrary, they waged continual and ferocious war upon one another with such fierceness that they did not consider victory at all worthwhile unless they satisfied their monstrous hunger with the flesh of their perfect enemies."[14]

Jesuit missionaries, organized according to a rigid hierarchy commanded by a "general," certainly constituted one of the most effective instruments in the spread of Christianity beyond the boundaries of the Old World, as well as a pillar of the Counter-Reformation. The order, known as the Society of Jesus, was founded by Saint Ignatius of Loyola (1491–1556) for the purpose of establishing a militia in service to the pope for the spread of Christianity and the defense of the church; the rule was approved verbally by Pope Paul III in 1540. Over time the reputation of the Jesuits as a "Machiavellian" order became so widespread, with the order's plotting and scheming, that in the seventeenth century a false Jesuit text, the *Monita privata*, appeared in Europe that claimed to contain the "secret instructions" to all Jesuits to gather riches to devote to the Society of Jesus's cunning and devious plan to conquer the world.[15]

"Sometimes the greatest wisdom is not knowing or pretending not to know," noted the Jesuit Baltasar Gracián, a sixteenth-century Spanish philosopher who devoted most of his works to teaching his readers how to navigate the shark-infested waters of a society where appearances rule over truth.[16] This is particularly true for those in power, and in works of his such as *El politico* (The politician), Gracián portrayed Philip IV, king of Spain, and princes and politicians as exemplary models of complete perfection, capable of such excellent qualities as prudence and acuity. However, precisely because of the considerable political influence that they had attained among numerous courts in Europe, the Jesuits became the targets of persecution, to the point that they were expelled during the seventeenth century from nearly all states and the order was suppressed in 1773 (it was rehabilitated by Pope Pius VII in 1814).

"In the early days of the Spanish colonial undertaking in the New World," writes Carlo Cipolla (1922–2000), an Italian economic historian, "the gold that the conquistadores obtained was exclusively the product of robbery and plunder. . . . With all that silver lying around it was only natural that the Spanish would hurl themselves, with all their love and enthusiasm for gold and silver, into the mining business."[17] And so it was that over the course of the sixteenth century the colonies "flooded Spain with more than 16,000 metric tons of silver, which then left awash with silver first Spain then one country after another," giving rise to an impressive development of commerce that was fraught with consequences for the entire continent of the Old World. And likewise, of course, for the New World, as we will see from the stories we are about to read of the new philosophical impulse that seems to root even more deeply in modern states, the age-old phenomenon of corruption, and the moral rebellion destined to result in the foundation of a future superpower.

SIX PHILOSOPHY OF CORRUPTION

France between Absolutism and Revolution, from Richelieu to Talleyrand (by Way of Robespierre)

THE SEVENTEENTH CENTURY in France was when the art of political corruption attained its peak, or at the very least enjoyed for the first time something on the order of a sort of philosophical theorization. But it was also the century of moralism par excellence. Corruption was perhaps more clearly stigmatized, but it also was given something like a certificate of inevitability. "If it is true that there is no way to annihilate sin, the art of those who govern is to ensure that it encourages the public weal," the moralist Marquis de Vauvenargues would write in the mid-eighteenth century.[1]

Between the sixteenth and eighteenth centuries, the concept of self-interest established itself not only as the principal paradigm of collective and individual experiences and customs, but also as one of the principal forms of legitimacy of the acts of the government. It was approved or opposed by the greatest writers of the time, from Machiavelli, La Rochefoucauld, Guicciardini, Hobbes, Spinoza, and Rousseau to Montaigne, Voltaire, Montesquieu, and Botero. Perhaps also for this reason we find among the leading protagonists of the century in France under King Louis XIV of France, the Sun King (1638–1715), a number of particularly powerful superintendents of finance. Characters like Nicolas Fouquet, who was put on trial for corruption and treason by Louis XIV, and his successor, Jean-Baptiste Colbert, would stand out in the biographical works written some three centuries later by the novelist Paul Morand (1888–1976). With the benefit of hindsight, the explanation for the necessary accumulation of personal property appears almost inevitable: "Fouquet," writes Morand, "must have believed that everything could be purchased, including destiny."[2] Fouquet was caught, just like the others and no more than them, in the infernal circle of his predecessors: Antoine d'Effiat, of whom Gédéon Tallemant des Réaux says in his *Les Historiettes* that he taught all those who came after him how to steal; Claude de Bullion, minister of finance under Louis XIII and founder of the Jardin des Plantes, whose loveliest plant was his own fortune, as it had grown far more and bloomed far more nicely than any of the other plants; Particelli, who was resourceful and unscrupulous, one of those countless shady Italians who followed in Cardinal Mazarin's entourage.

"The real harm," Morand goes on to say, "came not from the country's poverty, but from the lack of a Finance

Ministry. In the absence of a Bank of France, the state turned to private bankers. Now those bankers did not lend to the king unless the superintendent was rich enough to serve as collateral on behalf of the penniless king; if the superintendent was powerful, and, moreover, a parliamentary like Fouquet, the financiers were willing to give him credit. In this way, Fouquet made loans as a private citizen and repaid them as an administrator."[3] Jean-Baptiste Colbert, a protégé of Cardinal Mazarin, was left in charge of the cardinal's vast fortunes when he was briefly forced into exile from France in 1651. It seems he was good at it, for two years later, when Mazarin returned to France, he made Colbert administrator of his whole—and by then even larger—patrimony. Although Colbert was quite greedy, one of his first notable acts, which would many years later "enchant" Stendhal, was to turn down a gift of a thousand *écus* offered him by the cardinal.

Mazarin, on his deathbed, recommended Colbert to King Louis XIV, in spite of his quite unscrupulous ways. Morand writes: "[Colbert] buys an office and immediately turns around and sells it at a profit; he needs a regiment for one of his brothers, the supervision of the ships seized by corsairs for a cousin, a benefice for one of his sons. And now we see him as a candidate for the office of superintendent of the birdcages of the Tuileries; the offices he cannot keep he sells off, on his own behalf or for Mazarin, to whom he writes: 'For your offices of intendant I have found no purchasers willing to settle the deal at twelve thousand écus; I'm offering them for sale on all hands.' "[4]

Between the sixteenth and seventeenth centuries, the principle of absolutism affirmed itself in conjunction with the birth of the modern state, based substantially upon the practice of the centralization of political and military power, and characterized by a radical shift in equilibrium in favor of a growing and unlimited increase in the might of the monarchy. Its best-known theorization can be found in the *Six Books of the Commonwealth*, by Jean Bodin, who states that there are no limits to the will of the prince, save perhaps the laws of God and nature, and not even his own laws may serve to bind him. This is the opposite of what Huig Van Groot, known as Grotius, maintained in *De jure belli ac pacis* (On the law of war and peace). There he states that governments are not established for the benefit of those who rule but rather for the good of their subjects, hence that it is necessary to place limits, *de jure potestatis* (according to the law), in order to construct a valid regime for every country in times of war or peace. The traditional incarnation of Bodin's theory can be found in such powerful men as Henry IV, Richelieu, and later Louis XIV.

In the absolutist Europe of the seventeenth century the problem of ethics seems to have been by and large set aside. What prevailed was realpolitik, and every state operated on the principle of self-interest, which, most of the time, was equivalent to the self-interest of the sovereign and his court, as Louis XIV himself wrote in *The Craft of Kingship*: "The interests of the state must come first. When one has the state in view, one is working for oneself. The good of the one makes the glory of the other."[5] In the king's rather disenchanted view of things, though, those who have power must needs fall prey to corruption, be they governors, soldiers, or landowners, for corruption is the way of things and going against the current is too hard even for the honest man. The remedy lies in a platonic government of philosophers, was the caustic observation of La Rochefoucauld (1613–1680), a writer with a taste for opposing power (first, Richelieu's, later, Mazarin's) who wrote: "The Philosophers' scorn of wealth was but their secret ambition to exalt their merit above fortune by deriding those blessings which Fate denied them."[6] He added, in his *Maxims*, "What we mistake for virtue is often no more than a concurrence of diverse actions and interests, which fortune, or industry, disposes to advantage." This applies everywhere, in France as well as the rest of Europe, for instance, in Spain or in seventeenth-century Italy under Spanish domination, as described by Alessandro Manzoni (1785–1873) in the novel *I Promessi sposi* (The betrothed). From the narrative reconstruction of the great Italian author emerges, among the abuses of the powerful and the thwarted marriages, the figure of Bartolomeo d'Aquino, one of the first modern profiteers and fixers, a financier who enriched himself by lending money to the state and obtaining repayment with privileges of various kinds: titles of nobility, public lands, and bonds of feudal servitude. It was not until 1646, when the Spanish viceroy realized that the state was teetering on the brink of bankruptcy, that a warrant was issued for d'Aquino's arrest. Even then, the arrest never took place because of the development of "bureaucratic complications."

But for a classic case of financial skullduggery we are entirely justified in going back to France, where in 1716 John Law founded the Banque Royale, which was destined to solve, at least according to its proponent's intentions, the problem of the debts left by Louis XIV. The Banque Royale issued banknotes that would be used for daily expenses but that could be redeemed for metal coinage. The convertibility of the paper money would theoretically be guaranteed by the gold deposits in the American region of Louisiana, part of New France, exploited by the Mississippi Company, whose shares were in turn put on the market, where they sold like hotcakes. A bargain at the price to all appearances, until doubts began to spread about the very existence of the rich gold mines, and people began to ask to redeem their banknotes for gold. At that point a halt was put to the redemption of banknotes and many of the investors were ruined. The combination banknotes–stock shares closely resemble many of the most daring financial instruments and derivatives still fashionable today, all of which share a common characteristic found in market bubbles: the construction of a theoretical basis for profit built on castles in the sky. Just as there was no gold in Louisiana, likewise in the United States many centuries later nothing was known about the actual state of indebtedness of the companies controlled by Enron prior to its bankruptcy, because attentive and respected accounting firms actually conspired to conceal the truth. This is the same speculative folly that in the 1640s dragged the Netherlands into the craze called Tulipmania, until tulip bulbs were being valued at prices equal to that of the finest diamonds.

Voltaire describes the exploits of John Law as follows: "Within the last twenty years commerce has been better understood in France than it had ever before been, from the reign of Pharamond to that of Louis XIV. Before this period it was a secret art, a kind of chemistry in the hands of three or four persons, who actually made gold, but without communicating the secret by which they had been enriched. . . . It was destined that a Scotchman called John Law should come into France and overturn the whole economy of our government to instruct us."[7]

The prevalence of self-interest over all principles of honesty is a point of view carried to excess by the skeptical and nonconformist Bernard de Mandeville, who at the turn of the eighteenth century wrote an instructive and popular work called *The Fable of the Bees; Or, Private Vices and Public Benefits*, intended to show that a cynical government is the best possible government. When ruling over "Sharpers, Parasites, Pimps, Players, Pick-pockets, Coiners, Quacks, South-sayers," a corrupt government produces wealth and advantageous opportunities for one and all. The selfishness and passions thus derived, Mandeville claims, constitute the spring of welfare, while the virtues of man for the most part inhibit civil progress. To undermine this order can be fatal: "The building Trade is quite destroy'd, Artificers are not employ'd; . . . The Courtier's gone, that with his Miss Supp'd at his House on Christmas Peas; Spending as much in two Hours stay, As keeps a Troop of Horse a Day."[8] Wealth, in Mandeville's moral fable, is the child of vice, not virtue. What really drives a society forward is corruption, compromise, prostitution, and the absence of scruples. The civilizations that prohibit robbery and greed are destined to perish and languish over the centuries until they die out entirely. The economy, Mandeville reiterates, needs a continuous flow of artificial incentives, which it can never obtain by virtue alone, and it is a sign of folly to complain about the flourishing of vice if you want to enjoy the privileges and luxuries of an affluent life. "Bare

Virtue can't make Nations live In Splendor; they, that would revive A Golden Age, must be as free, For Acorns, as for Honesty."

In that case, why show contempt for the contribution of corruption to social progress? Why discount the role of corruption as the engine of the world? This lesson was stated with greater equanimity at a later date by the liberal historian and statesman Alexis de Tocqueville: "The principle of interest rightly understood," wrote the author in *Democracy in America*,

> perhaps prevents some men from rising far above the level of mankind; but a great number of other men, who were falling far below it, are caught and restrained by it. Observe some few individuals, they are lowered by it; survey mankind, it is raised. I am not afraid to say that the principle of interest, rightly understood, appears to me the best suited of all philosophical theories to the wants of the men of our time, and that I regard it as their chief remaining security against themselves. Towards it, therefore, the minds of the moralists of our age should turn. . . . Nevertheless I cannot believe that all those who practise virtue from religious motives are only actuated by the hope of a recompense. I do not believe that interest is the sole motive of religious men: but I believe that interest is the principal means which religions themselves employ to govern men, and I do not question that this way they strike into the multitude and become popular.[9]

In fact, the French Revolution of 1789—leaving aside any and all historical interpretations or reconstructions—

clearly showed that it was not possible to eliminate corruption of the Crown and of the First and Second Estates except through the rise of new forms of public and private malfeasance, leading to the birth of new subjects engaging in the same phenomenon. The incorruptible Robespierre was guillotined once the Terror had devastated Paris and France. And it is strangely daunting to read how Robespierre's sister described her brother's naïve moralism in the presence of a well-known turncoat: "Fouché, after having been introduced to me by my brother, came to see me assiduously, and had those regards and attentions that one has for a person in whom one is particularly interested. Fouché was not handsome, but he had a charming wit and was extremely amiable. He spoke to me of marriage, and I admit that I felt no repugnance for that bond, and that I was well enough disposed to accord my hand to [him] whom my brother had introduced to me as a pure democrat and his friend. I did not know that Fouché was only a hypocrite, a swindler, a man without convictions, without morals, and capable of doing anything to satisfy his frenzied ambition. He knew so well how to disguise his vile sentiments and his malicious passions in my eyes as in my brother's eyes, that I was his dupe as well as Maximilien. I responded to his proposition that I wanted to think about it and consult my brother, and I asked him the time to resolve myself. I spoke of it, effectively, to Robespierre, who showed no opposition to my union with Fouché."[10]

"You have accepted no money," the German playwright Georg Büchner (1813–1837), in *Danton's Death*, has Danton say to Robespierre: "You have contracted no debts, you have slept with no women, you always wear a respectable coat, and you never get drunk. Robespierre, you are appallingly virtuous. I would be ashamed to mince along between Heaven and earth for thirty years, making the same moral face, simply for the miserable satisfaction of finding everyone else nastier than me. . . . You're so virtuous that, to you, life itself is a sin. You and your virtue. Robespierre!"[11]

Robespierre himself stated in his speech to the French National Convention on February 5, 1794, that "the soul of the Republic is virtue," and there can be no doubt that for the revolutionary leader the most absolute evil was incarnated by an absolute monarchy. Mentioning the example of Richelieu, he wrote: "With such shamelessness, they pass laws against theft, though they themselves plunder the public coffers. In their name murderers are condemned and they murder millions of men with their wars."[12]

Nicolas de Condorcet (1743–1794), the philosopher who was Girondin deputy to the Legislative Assembly and the National Convention—he was arrested during the Terror and committed suicide in his cell—recalled that Mirabeau one day suggested to the financier Jacques Necker that they govern France together, even though they did not see eye to eye in matters of public expense. But Necker replied curtly: "Your strength is politics; mine is morality. Clearly we could never get along."[13] Revolutions pass, but people remain unchanged.

Napoleon Bonaparte (1769–1821) was accustomed to telling his ministers that they were free to steal a little, as long as they ran efficient administrations. Charles Maurice de Talleyrand-Périgord (1754–1838), better known as the prince of Talleyrand, certainly didn't go down in history as an evildoer for having worn, over the course of his life, a number of coats of different colors: loyal servant of Louis XVI, foreign minister under the Directory, adviser to Bonaparte, and also his sworn enemy as the French plenipotentiary at the Congress of Vienna. Quite the contrary, his devotion to the cause of politics and the generosity with which he put his diplomatic gifts at the service of opposing causes are if anything still today the object of considerable admiration. Even in the judgment of Napoleon himself, who considered him a traitor and a turncoat—in short, a man too prudent and too systematically fortunate to really be honest—there is a clear note of respect when he states that the only way to get anything from Talleyrand is to pay him. Napoleon in effect implies that the man always had something worth obtaining. At a dear price.

And indeed, Talleyrand, the prince of international negotiations, always skillfully managed to pilfer money from foreign powers in exchange for a tractable position during the back and forth of diplomacy, a game that worked both with the old European monarchies and with the nascent democracy of the United States. The French writer and politician François-René de Chateaubriand (1768–1848) listed a number of Talleyrand's "successes": "By the million which he received from Portugal in the hope of a signature of peace with the Directory, a peace which was never signed; by the purchase of Belgian bonds on the Peace of Amiens, of which he, M. de Talleyrand, knew before it was known to the public; by the erection of the short-lived kingdom of Etruria; by the secularization of the ecclesiastical properties of Germany; by the jobbing of his opinions at the Congress of Vienna."[14] But he was probably more "enlightened" than many revolutionaries, if it is true that he was a strenuous defender of mandatory public education and an assiduous defender of the freedom of the press, in particular during the period of the restoration in Europe.

If political intelligence, philosophical speculation, and diffuse corruption dominated pre- and post-revolutionary France, on the other side of the Channel a very similar mixture was helping the British to build an empire.

SEVEN A PRAGMATIC APPROACH TO CORRUPTION

England in the Industrial Revolution

IN BRITAIN, more or less in the same historical period, the seventeenth to eighteenth centuries, an increasingly defined notion of corruption seems to have established itself, just as it was happening in France. This notion was accompanied by a pragmatic approach to the subject, typical of the tradition of Anglo-Saxon thought. It has been said that the founding fathers of British power—Francis Bacon, a philosopher and statesman; Samuel Pepys, a naval administrator; and Warren Hastings, one of the creators of British India—contentedly accepted bribes and never felt a twinge of shame in their souls. And yet the British Empire, in its vast and progressive diffusion, would also prove to be an effective tool for spreading throughout the world a diametrically opposed ethical conception regarding corruption, thanks especially to the role played by the migratory waves of Puritans to North America and the exportation to those lands of their creed.

In 1621 the English parliament brought charges of corruption against Sir Francis Bacon, then lord chancellor of the kingdom. He was thought to be guilty of taking bribes through intermediaries in exchange for favorable decisions from the chancellery. Even though some sources consider it possible that he was simply made a scapegoat in revenge for the attacks he launched against the Duke of Buckingham, Bacon admitted his guilt and chose not to mount a defense. He was fined £40,000 and sentenced to prison, although he managed to avoid that fate because of his excellent relations with King James I.

In his defense on these charges Bacon made a distinction between the "donations" he received before and after the decisions in question were made, maintaining that the donations made after the decision could not have altered the course of the law. He also reminded his judges that a distinction should be made between the "vices of the time" and the "vices of man." He seemed to be saying that the practice of taking bribes was de facto accepted within the fabric of British society, even if it was clearly not accepted in more abstract terms in the body of law then in effect. In other words, Bacon asserted, all periods have their customs. He compared the laws to spider webs, useful for catching flies but bound to let horseflies get through. In other words, we might say nowadays, using a different animal metaphor, they catch the small fry while, in the venues where corruption runs rampant, the big fish break the net, swim through, and grow fat with impunity. Over the centuries the chief defense continued to be *così fan tutti*. From Verres to Nixon the basic problem is always the same.

In 1668, Samuel Pepys (1633–1703), who would later become secretary to the British Admiralty, was the focus of a parliamentary inquiry that put his activities under the microscope. Pepys was a prominent official and a notably efficient one, an expert in bureaucratic matters, an authentic master of the art of contracts and of managing relations with the providers of countless raw materials, capable of solving problems when they arose, and particularly fond of receiving gifts of all kinds: animals, clothing, food, items in silver, and cash. What makes him even today an interesting topic of study is the impressively meticulous way in which he recorded, day by day, his work and especially the numerous gifts that oiled the administrative machinery that he himself managed—gifts of oysters, gloves filled with gold, sturgeons, and, more simply, cash payments.

On March 25, 1663, Pepys wrote: "This evening came Captain Grove about hiring ships for Tangier. I did hint to him my desire that I could make some lawfull profit thereof, which he promises that he will tell me of all that he gets and that I shall have a share, which I did not demand, but did silently consent to it, and money I perceive something will be got thereby."[1] In this entry it is clear that the system of "tacit taxation" was so widespread and accepted that it could be taken in relatively good faith as a legitimate form of behavior. Pepys had taken the main road indicated by his protector, Admiral Sir Edward Montague (Earl of Sandwich), and he challenged the prosecution to prove that he had actually pocketed anything other than what he was owed for his services. As a confirmation of his tactics, Pepys's trial ended with his acquittal, in part because what he wrote in his diary, though rendered public, was never confirmed by those involved; and in part because Pepys had powerful friends and was protected by King Charles II, who made sure that the case would culminate in the defendant's dismissal. An acquittal that was probably reinforced Pepys's own belief that he had been in the right, because he continued to consider the bribe as a perfectly legitimate commission due him, a simple percentage on business procured.

A realistic and effective picture of corruption in eighteenth-century British society can be obtained from the splendid engravings of one of the fathers of caricature, William Hogarth (1697–1764). Among his creations are depictions of scenes from an election campaign in the aptly named Guzzletown, inspired by the real-life episode of the unexpected Whig victory in 1754 in a traditionally Tory district in Oxfordshire.

But there was certainly no lack of material for those interested in satirizing the aristocracy and the government. The *Beggar's Opera*, by John Gay (1685–1732), targeted the powerful who clothed themselves in fine principles; yet this cast of characters was in fact played by thieves, fences, painted ladies, lawyers, and policemen conniving to shake down for cash anyone who looks like a good mark. Gay's play gained later fame in part due to its free adaptation by Bertolt Brecht for his *Threepennny Opera*. The twentieth-century German writer Brecht (1898–1956) preserved the names of the original characters (the bandit Captain Macheath, the fence Jonathan Jeremiah Peachum, his daughter, Polly Peachum), even as he shifted the action to London in the early twentieth century, a universe just as teeming with paupers, thieves, and prostitutes as the seventeenth, where the loan shark and fence Peachum tries unsuccessfully to send his unwanted son-in-law, Mackie Messer, to the gallows, in a succession of plot twists, betrayals, and escapes. The original inspiration for both John Gay and Bertolt Brecht—and also Henry Fielding and Daniel Defoe—was the authentic and extraordinary criminal Jonathan Wild, who was probably the best-known figure in the English underworld of the entire seventeenth century: a bandit and an informant, corrupt and corrupting, but also, when it was for his own personal benefit, a servant of the law. Over an ample span of time, Wild managed to manipulate the press and remain on good terms with the police, even as he led his gang of thieves in a series of stunning knockovers. A key element of his technique was to hand over to authorities on a regular basis the names of adversaries or two-bit crooks. He thus avoided trouble with the law for many years.

In 1712 the Whig MP and secretary of war Robert Walpole was expelled from the British parliament on charges of corruption. He returned under George I as first lord of the treasury, and later as chancellor of the exchequer and minister of finance (he thus created for the first time the office of prime minister). Among his fiercest adversaries was William Pitt the Elder, who in turn became prime minister, and accused Walpole of looking on with complacency and incompetence as the affairs of the nation suffered while he cultivated his own private interests. With his harangues Pitt contributed to the fall of Walpole's government. In an age when separating corruption and political manipulation from "simple" politics was as difficult as it is today, Walpole left his mark as a peculiarly manipulative man of power. In the eighteenth-century ballad "The Knight and the Prelate," a satire on the government in the form of a mock conference between Sir Robert Walpole (the knight) and Edmund Gibson, bishop of London (the prelate), it is said of Walpole that "he judged of Men's Worth by the Weight of their Fee."

Another fierce opponent of Walpole's policies was Lord Bolingbroke (1678–1751), a leading Tory who was the secretary of war and foreign minister. Politician that he was, he had a certain dose of realism if it is true that he left it written that "to preserve liberty by new laws and new schemes of government, whilst the corruption of people continues and grows, is absolutely impossible."[2] In twenty years of his "reign" over England, Walpole enriched himself immensely, precisely through his very pragmatic policies of a great balancing of powers, both at home and abroad. In fact, it is quite likely that we can find a portrait of him in the pages of Jonathan Swift's *Gulliver's Travels* in the character of Flimnap, the great treasurer of the empire of Lilliput, where high offices are assigned in accordance with courtiers' skills at dancing on a very thin rope. And Flimnap "is allowed to cut a caper on the straight rope, at least an inch higher than any other lord in the whole empire." He does happen to fall, this much is true, but he lands gently on the king's cushion.

If the highest offices in government were held by men willing to turn a blind and complacent eye to the offer of a moderate bribe, we shouldn't think, however, that in seventeenth-century England voices were not also raised against the practice. Unfortunately, those voices were not particularly effective. One inquisitor of great rectitude who lambasted the decline of the mores among the powerful was Edmund Burke, a conservative historian and a white-hot polemicist of the period. Among his choice targets: the renowned Warren Hastings, former clerk of the British East India Company and the first governor of India, who was charged in the second half of the eighteenth century with malfeasance and corruption and returned to England in 1785 to be tried. Hastings had no problems with admitting he had taken sizable bribes, but he candidly explained that the money had basically been used to the company's advantage. The trial lasted many years and ended with Hastings's acquittal by the House of Lords—indeed, with the defendant's ultimate glorification. In short, the rewards of vice. Meanwhile the rewards of virtue are quickly summed up: In the aftermath of the case, the "censorious" Burke came to be considered by a substantial portion of public opinion a sick man who was eaten up with his persecutory obsession. Disappointed by the outcome of the trial, Burke came to the conclusion that the only possible solution was to entrust himself and Hastings both to divine justice, the only kind destined to endure. "There is one thing, and one thing only, which defies all mutation; that which existed before the world, and will survive the fabrick of the world itself; I mean Justice; that justice which, emanating from the Divinity . . . will stand, after this globe is burned to ashes, our advocate or our accuser before the great Judge, when He comes to call upon us for the tenor of a well spent life."[3] But in spite of these pious hopes, Burke bitterly concluded that the chivalrous age in which it was possible to believe in the virtue of man was at an end, and now the stars of economists, sophists, and calculators shone brightest.

The poet Alexander Pope (1688–1744) had foreseen, "At length, Corruption, like a gen'ral flood / Shall deluge all; and Avarice creeping on / Spread like a low-born mist; and blot the Sun / Statesman and Patriot ply alike the stocks / Peeress and Butler share alike the Box / And Judges job, and Bishops bite the town / And mighty Dukes pack cards for half a crown. / See Britain sunk in lucre's sordid charms."[4] Perhaps Pope was a victim of 1711's South Sea Bubble.

Before Great Britain could sink into the slime of its own corruption, a group of patriots fled toward new coasts. Or, perhaps we should say, toward the coasts of a new world.

EIGHT THE AMERICAN DREAM OF PURITY

From the Moralizing Promise of the Mayflower
to the Triumph of the Gangsters

IN 1621, a group of a hundred or so English immigrants
aboard the *Mayflower* landed at Cape Cod in North
America and founded the Plymouth colony. Among them
were the Pilgrim fathers who had chosen the path of exile
and a reestablishment of their community in a new continent, not only due to their hostility to the Anglican
Church but also in the name of ideals of purity that they
believed were long lost in their homeland. The hope of
creating a society free of corruption found its foundations
in particular in the Mayflower Compact, signed on the
ship and subscribed by forty-one male passengers—a social contract that can be considered an embryonic document of the birth of the United States: It staked a claim on

the possibility of moral rebirth that still animates American political debate and rhetoric.

When they were debating the makeup of the Constitution of the United States, the Founding Fathers Benjamin Franklin and Thomas Jefferson had on their bedside tables *The Decline and Fall of the Roman Empire*, by Edward Gibbon, published in 1776, the year of the Declaration of Independence. Among the Latin writers that we know they read were Tacitus and Cicero, in whose narratives corruption certainly occupied a central place; it was presented as the principal political adversary of the republic as well as one of the causes of the fall of the greatest empire of antiquity. In the eyes of the members of the American Constitutional Convention corrupt ancient Rome resembled the hated Great Britain, whose parliamentarians always seemed eager and willing to surrender their own liberty, along with the principles and the interests of the community they represented, in exchange for the money or privileges given to them by the current monarch.

For that very reason, in the Articles of Confederation of 1777 it is stated that no person who holds public office in the service of the United States can receive any kind of interested gift. And the Constitution reiterated the point even more decisively, in Article 1, Section 9, with the specification that the "emolument, Office, or Title, of any kind whatever" could not be accepted "without the Consent of the Congress." And so it was that when Benjamin Franklin, when he departed from Paris in 1785 after having served American interests in France for many years, received an exquisite diamond-encrusted tobacco box with a portrait of Louis XIV, there was an immediate assumption that accepting the gift would be tantamount to corruption. Not until Congress specifically issued authorization was Franklin allowed to take possession of the object he had been given (his daughter ignored her father's instructions and sold the diamonds to pay for a trip to Europe).

Thomas Jefferson, even though he called for "honesty, truth, temperance" and "a wise and frugal Government" in his inaugural address, behaved quite differently when he received a similar gift at the end of his diplomatic service in Paris. He gave his secretary instructions to sell the diamonds in order to pay his office expenses, without contacting Congress in advance to request permission. In formal terms, at least, he was basically giving a minor but meaningful signal of a relaxed approach to the very rules that he had helped to establish.

In the meantime, other measures were taken in an effort to limit corruption, but gifts from a foreign king to a diplomat clearly constituted only one of many possible instances of malfeasance on the part of a public official, and there still was a lack of a broader definition of what constituted a violation. The Anti-Federalists, led by George Mason at the Constitutional Convention in Philadelphia in 1787, during the process of debating and ratifying the Constitution, had warned in the strongest terms of the risk the country faced of becoming corrupt if it had a strong centralized government in which the president held the power to tax and to veto congressional legislation. They insisted on a bill of rights that granted individual liberties to all U.S. citizens. But the risk of corruption didn't end with the government. Corruption could occur anywhere in the political or administrative structures.

A particularly clear example is the case of the political machine known as Tammany Hall. "Tammany" is derived from the name of a Native American leader, but it acquired immediate recognition as a shorthand for bribes, graft, and illicit favors in the context of nineteenth- and early-twentieth-century U.S. politics. Founded in 1786 in New York as an organization with social scope, it soon became a political and electoral machine strictly tied to the Democratic Party, helping to control the city and the state of New York from the end of the eighteenth century. Its patronage system ensured it control of the votes of the great and growing number of Irish Catholic immigrants. The most infamous leader of Tammany was perhaps William M "Boss" Tweed (1823–1878), who became president of the Democratic Party in New York County in 1860 and was accused (and convicted in 1871) of seizing tens of millions of dollars from the public coffers. Tammany's role of buying votes and controlling public expenditures continued virtually unchecked until 1930, and gave its last gasp in 1960.

Robert Morris (1734–1806) provides another example of extra-governmental corruption in U.S. history. Morris, a friend of George Washington, was a rich entrepreneur who was the owner of a shipping-banking-real estate company based in Philadelphia. He had a central role as "financer of the Revolution" and in helping the Continental Army and Navy against the British. But he missed no opportunity to advance his own affairs. As superintendent of finance he became, from 1781 to 1784, one of the most powerful men in the new United States, lending money to states in difficult financial situation, but he was soon accused by Thomas Paine of profiteering from his position in the government. He was simultaneously a patriot and a profiteer, who genuinely served the cause of the Revolution but also channeled assets in his own direction. Ultimately his was a grand fall: he lost the fortune he had accumulated by speculating on lands of the frontier and elsewhere in a bankruptcy that landed him in jail for some time. He died in obscurity.[1]

Land speculation was a fertile ground for corruption and self-dealing in the new country. One renowned land fraud case is known as Yazoo. The scandal first exploded in 1795, in Georgia, where cases of speculation teemed around the various state landholdings, which were particularly numerous and whose boundaries in some cases were uncertain. Certain profiteers managed to influence their political representatives so as to arrange to be sold at very favorable prices state-owned lands, later subject to appealing forms of exploitation. The politician Patrick Henry founded the Virginia Yazoo Company, which took its name from the river that ran across the land in question. Many state legislators invested in it. This made it very much in their own interest to approve the sale of public lands to the company, which they promptly proceeded to do without worrying overmuch about the conflicts of interest involved.

The real estate investment that Henry made was, according to many observers, one of the most profitable in the entire history of the country, at least for those lucky enough to be among the speculators. It aroused the indignation of a great many citizens and led to the founding of an "anti-Yazoo" movement that succeeded in winning the next elections and came dangerously close to killing the deal by voting to annul it because of the fraud that underlay it. But the company, supported politically by those who believed that a contract made by free citizens could not be legally invalidated, continued to sell the lands thus acquired. The matter came before Congress, where a committee was created that included Secretary of State James Madison. When it concluded its hearings, the committee established that the initial sale voted by the Georgia assembly was null and void, but it made no clear final decision concerning similar practices undertaken in other parts of the country.

In 1810, Robert Fletcher, a citizen of New Hampshire, purchased land in the Yazoo from a Massachusetts citizen, John Peck, but shortly thereafter Fletcher accused Peck of not actually holding the necessary deeds of ownership to the land. This case made its way all the way up to the Supreme Court, which was presided over by Justice John Marshall—who, curiously enough, had been implicated in a prior episode of real estate speculation. The verdict established that in theory the initial legislative action of the state of Georgia in selling the land to the Yazoo Company might have been invalid, but that any original corruption could have no subsequent consequences on a contract between two private citizens. Marshall added that the courts can have no jurisdiction to judge legislation legitimately approved by a state assembly, even if that approval sprang from alleged cases of corruption. Needless to say, the case of *Fletcher* v. *Peck* had significant and lasting consequences in the struggle against political corruption in the United States.

With economic growth came the era of the great railroad swindles, whose general scheme to some extent mirrors the "Yazoo mechanism": Congress appropriated close to $2 billion in present-day money which it paid to private citizens who pledged they would cover the country with railroads. These people in turn sold shares in their companies to congressmen in order to make sure they could count on continuous support and only limited oversight into the significant expenses that the infrastructures they were building had accumulated. Among the politicians involved in these operations was the notoriously ruthless Oakes Ames, a Republican from Massachusetts and a major investor in the Union Pacific Railroad and Crédit Mobilier, who sold shares in these companies at below-market prices to members of Congress. The investigation into accusations against him of corruption failed to find that there had been any criminal conduct. Certainly it was one of the low points in the battle against corruption in the history of the United States.

After years without regulations on finance in politics and election campaigns, something finally began to change with the growing distribution of the penny press, which in the first half of the nineteenth century began to focus on politics in a critical manner, in compliance with the interests of readers eager to learn of scandals and sensationalist stories, in this field as well as others. Something similar happened with the campaign of Andrew Jackson (in office 1829–1837), who for the first time tried to mobilize voters actively, organizing lecture tours, writing pamphlets, and calling on the press to be involved, and also encouraged the introduction of systems of rotation in public offices, directed at ending the tendency to fall into the temptation of bribery. Some fifty years later the presidential candidate James Garfield (1831–1881), who had promised to do battle on this front, was killed shortly after the election by a man who believed he was owed a government position. In the aftermath of the assassination, the Pendleton Act was passed, which introduced meritocratic criteria in civil service hiring with the purpose of eliminating the old party-based "spoils system." The act made it far more difficult to offer positions as blandishments during election campaigns, and began to place some initial limitations on funds raised for electoral purposes.

Still, American election campaigns between the end of the nineteenth century and the beginning of the twentieth century remained very expensive and unregulated. Intimidation remained widespread and the secret ballot was only introduced gradually. The Democratic candidate, William Jennings Bryan, although he was supported by such influential men as William Randolph Hearst, was easily beaten by his opponent, William McKinley, who could count on the support of Mark Hanna (1837–1904), a senator and businessman from Ohio. Hanna, both unscrupulous and self-interested, was one of the wealthiest men in the nation. He managed to impose a sort of tax on banks sufficient to ensure the necessary funds, and therefore the necessary influence, to ensure that his protégé, McKinley, would win not one but two presidential elections. When McKinley was assassinated at a public event in 1901, his place was taken by his vice president, Teddy Roosevelt, formerly the New York City police commissioner, who was determined finally to lay the foundations of a legal system capable of fighting the spreading epidemic of corruption. In a 1903 speech, Roosevelt denounced political corruption as a crime worse than murder because it spreads its evil effects not only to a single person but the entire commonwealth.[2] As a result, he encouraged prosecutors for the first time to go after cases of political corruption. He then went on to strongly support, with the Tillman Act, the first political finance reform, which made donations from corporations illegal for federal campaigns and required candidates to document their spending with a certain degree of transparency. Later, the Federal Corrupt Practices Act, enacted in 1910 by President William H. Taft, placed specific limits on spending for all general elections for the House of Representatives and obliged political parties to disclose all details of their expenditures in post-electoral reports.

Roosevelt also was the first to deploy the Sherman Anti-Trust Act in a meaningful way. Directed against the excessive power of economic monopolies and industrial cartels, the act, passed in 1890, was the first antitrust legislation in the United States.

It also appears evident that moralizing campaigns that originated with the finest of intentions can bring about significant collateral damage. This was the case of Prohibition, when the production, commerce, and retail sale of alcohol was forbidden, in the early decades of the twentieth century, a decision that unleashed one of the greatest waves of organized crime in American history, with the rise of powerful gangsters and the systematic corruption of public offices in charge of enforcing the anti-alcohol laws.

In 1946 the Hobbs Act went into effect, a reform against organized crime that in its subsequent interpretations was used to restrict forms of extortion and dismantle bribery-driven government machinery that availed itself of the complicity of public officials. But the real turning point in the fight against corruption wouldn't come until many years later, as an unintended consequence of the Watergate Scandal in 1972, which started with the illegal wire-tapping of the offices of the Democratic Party and ended with the impeachment of President Richard Nixon, who had tried to suppress his involvement in the break-in and the cover-up. The reforms passed in 1974, intended to strengthen the rules of the Federal Election Campaign Act of 1971, introduced public campaign financing, forbade contributions above a certain cap, and created oversight agencies.

The end of corruption in America? One could hope, but in vain. Meanwhile, in the Old World, corruption had taken on new and terrifying faces.

NINE RESTORATION AND DECADENCE

Bourgeoisie and Bureaucracy, Corruption between Modern Capitalism and the Nation-State

IT IS SAID THAT the Duke of Wellington could never have paid his army at the Battle of Waterloo without the helping hand, or the wallet, of the Rothschilds. The Rothschild bank, owned by Nathan Rothschild (1777–1836) of Frankfurt, featured on its coat of arms the protective wings of an eagle emblazoned on a red shield, the same sign that the founder of the Rothschild dynasty had first placed over the front door of his first shop when he was a goldsmith. After Wellington's victory, Rothschild won the contract to manage the payment of tributes to the European allies. In Italy, the Count of Cavour (1810–1861) prepared to pursue the Second War of Independence against Austria with funds he obtained from the House of Rothschild using the excuse that he planned to use the money to build the Mont Cenis Pass Railway, the first mountain railway in the world. Indeed, up until 1880, the House of Rothschild actually did underwrite the construction of a substantial portion of the railroads of Europe.

In the nineteenth century, in part with the emergence of such major banking dynasties as the Rothschilds, the relationship between money and power expanded to fit new definitions and outlooks, as well as continuing to constitute one of the cruxes of politics for countries and rulers. The principle underlying all economic activity is the absence of scruples, wrote the German economist and sociologist Werner Sombart (1863–1941) in his book *Der moderne Kapitalismus*; the ease with which money circulates makes corruption that much easier as the traces left by its passage from hand to hand become increasingly evanescent. In a harsh analysis of the role of colonialism in the genesis of modern capitalism, he clearly stated that "systematic exploitment of the Mediterranean peoples by way of forced labour was the basis on which the power of Venice and Genoa was built" and goes on to demonstrate that without the violations and corruption attendant on the colonial economic system, capitalism as we know it today would hardly be possible.[1] The equation money + violence = capitalism would become more and more firmly established. The German economist Georg Simmel (1858–1918), in his *Philosophy of Money*, blamed the inherent nature of money for this decay of moral values: "We experience in the nature of money itself something of the essence of prostitution. The indifference as to its use, the lack of attachment to any individual because it is unrelated to any of them, the objectivity inherent in money as a mere means which excludes any emotional relationship—all this produces an ominous analogy between money and prostitution."[2]

In 1918, on the eve of the collapse of imperial Germany, the still unknown philosopher Oswald Spengler published the first volume of the *The Decline of the West*, in whose apocalyptic pages he predicted the end of European civilization. The book was an immediate hit and the uproar was deafening. The "outlines of morphology of world history" indicated by Spengler gave a literary face to the crisis of bourgeois civilization that coincides with the last part of the four-season cycle of every civilization and of the ages of man as well: childhood, youth, manhood, and old age. The fresco of civilization at sunset would have one of its most successful depictions in Robert Musil's *The Man without Qualities*.

As in the past, this new twist in the history of corruption has its opponents. On such scourges of political mores was Richard von Schaukal (1874–1942), a Moravian-Austrian poet who was also a government functionary in Vienna. In his *The Life and Opinions of Herr Andreas Von Balthesser, Dandy and Dilettante* he fell back on positions verging on the platonic, insisting, "No one is better able to support the monarchic principle than the aristocrat whose blood is imbued with feudal duty."[3] For another Austrian writer, Joseph Roth, the end of the Austro-Hungarian empire and more generally the end of old order in Europe coincided to some extent with that of the von Trotta family in his novel *The Radetzky March*: Count Chojnicki had "for years now . . . been a deputy to the Imperial Council, routinely reelected by his district, beating all other candidates with the help of money, violence, and surprise attacks; a minion of the government, he despised the parliamentary body to which he belonged."[4]

Another renowned family from literature is that of the Buddenbrooks, an industrial German dynasty whose ineluctably declining trajectory Thomas Mann sketches with breathtaking mastery: "Framed in heavy, carved walnut and covered with glass were the portraits of the four owners of the firm of Johann Buddenbrook. . . . A stylized golden ear of grain twined its way among the portraits. . . . And above it all, written in the tall Gothic script of a hand familiar to his descendants, was the motto: 'My son, show zeal for each day's affairs of business, but only for such that make for a peaceful night's sleep.' "[5]

It is certainly no accident that a century in which money becomes global should have been characterized by an unprecedented expansionistic impulse on the part of the nation-states at the peak of their power. Among the greatest theorists of imperialism (before the numerous subsequent analyses in an economic context by such thinkers as John Hobson, Joseph Schumpeter, and Lenin, who published in 1916, in the midst of the Great War, *Imperialism, the Highest Stage of Capitalism*) we find the British statesman Benjamin Disraeli. As a Tory member of parliament, chancellor of the exchequer, and finally prime minister from 1874 to 1880, Disraeli sustained Britain's propensity for expansionism which ultimately led to the creation of a vast empire that by the early 1920s would count about one-fifth of the world's population as its subjects. There can be no doubt that Disraeli hoped to export a model of governance that was to some extent positive—he had declared that England's parliaments had become over the past fifty "less and less corrupt" and attributed the reason for that decline, remarkably, not to the parliaments themselves but rather to the role played by the press. "You may pass what laws you like," he declared in a speech to the House of Commons on June 20, 1848, "but the ultimate means by which intimidation and corruption will be repressed is by elevating the tone of public feeling, and bringing the influence of public opinion through the press to bear upon the conduct of the great body of the nation."[6]

In this case too, there was no shortage of voices raised in opposition. The Dutch author Eduard Douwes Dekker (1820–1887), who wrote under the pen name Multatuli, in the classic of Dutch literature *Max Havelaar*, denounced the violence inflicted by the colonialism of the Dutch in the East Indies. Other writers and commentators of the time made the same observations. It was precisely in the second half of the nineteenth century that Western colonialism, territorial expansion, and the intense economic exploitation of the countries of the Americas, Asia, and Africa reached their most intense phase. This colonialism, motivated by commercial and military considerations, was bolstered by racial and religious theories of the civil superiority of Old World cultures to those of the peoples colonized. Therefore, the theory went, they had a "moral obligation" to rule and Christianize the populations that were held to be so uncivilized. It is a full fledged divvying up of the "rest of the world" by the European powers, formally sanctioned at the Berlin Conference in 1884–1885. The consequences of colonialism were to prove enormous in scale and extremely long lasting: politically, from the attempt to impose western political models; economically, because of the spread and redistribution of agricultural crops around the world; and, in more general terms, culturally and demographically, as a result of the corruption of customs, ways of life, and indigenous social structures. One highly significant example of these deleterious effects was the radical exploitation of natural resources and human labor in the colony of the Congo Free State as a private colonial economic venture by King Leopold II of Belgium (1835–1909).

Cecil Rhodes, too, plundered a substantial portion of the part of Africa that was occupied by the British Empire. Rhodes's unscrupulous motto, as it happened, was "Every man has his price." The necessity of governing distant, foreign lands, on the one hand, and the distance from the central power—and control—on the other could hardly help but prove fertile terrain for a flourishing fauna of small-time corrupt functionaries, with the resulting spread of the practice of acquiring either a person's complicity, or his silence. For that matter, how could the outgrowths of the British Empire and European colonies around the globe ever hope to be more virtuous than the states they reported back to? It is understandable that Winston Churchill is said to have come up with a cynical description of the Tory party that includes the laconic axiom "Corruption at home, aggression abroad to cover it up."[7]

In *Nostromo*, the Polish-American writer Joseph Conrad (1857–1924) describes the personality of a mine director in the not excessively fictitious country of Costaguana in Latin America: "Charles Gould was competent because he had no illusions. The Gould Concession had to fight for life with such weapons as could be found at once in the mire of a corruption that was so universal as almost to lose its significance." Gould states, "I pin my faith to material interests. Only let the material interests once get a firm footing, and they are bound to impose the conditions on which alone they can continue to exist. That's how your money-making is justified here in the face of lawlessness and disorder."[8]

The "money complex," as we have seen and as we shall see to an even greater extent in the chapters that follow, is present in a vast portion of European literature, from Shakespeare's *The Merchant of Venice* to Chamisso's *Peter Schlemihls wundersame Geschichte* to Honoré de Balzac's cycle *La Comédie humaine*. Georg Simmel claims that a cash economy has the merit of freeing individuals from feudal relationships and servitude to the earthly clod and other physical objects, and this is no doubt true, but it hardly seems to replace the corruption of the social system of feudal societies with anything close to moral rectitude. The birth of capitalist society appears to have been capable of offering a limitless quantity of goods and services, by creating new needs and new and unscrupulous strategies to satisfy them, while at the same time encouraging a moralistic and often sterile contempt toward "the god money."

The nineteenth century was a time that focused intently upon money as a means of social affirmation and participation in political life in a major role; political influence would in turn make it possible to accumulate still more money. The character of Vautrin in *Père Goriot*, perhaps one of Balzac's most powerful creations, seems to summarize in some sense the spirit of the time. (Balzac based his character on the real-life story of Eugène-François Vidocq, who also inspired Victor Hugo. Vautrin also has characteristics similar to the protagonist of Alexandre Dumas's *The Count of Monte Cristo*.) The old convict sentenced to forced labor who becomes chief of the secret police possesses a certain intrinsic grandeur and was a constant interest of the author's: power is necessary because it is the last resource in the face of a morality undermined by decadence and corruption. In him and in the character Eugene Rastignac, Balzac seems to see the sole expressions—in a certain sense, triumphant and positive—of the society in which he lived, a triumph that is individual, ambiguous, painful, and provisional. The effort to subject people to reason, claims Balzac—is constant and lies at the foundation of any successful political action: "If thought, or if passion, which combines thought and feeling, is the vital social element, it is also its destructive element. In this respect social life is like the life of man. Nations live long only by moderating their vital energy."[9] It is no accident that Balzac should have attempted such an ambitious systematization of human behavior.

According to Victor Hugo, who lived in the same period, it was self-interest, more than passion, that directed the behavior of the voters. Who voted for Napoleon III, Hugo wonders. He answers his own question:

M. Bonaparte had for him the crowd of officeholders, the one million two hundred thousand parasites of the budget, and their dependents and hangers-on; the corrupt, the compromised, the adroit; and in their train the crétins, a very considerable party. He had for him Messieurs the Cardinals, Messieurs the Bishops, Messieurs the Canons, Messieurs the Curés, Messieurs the Vicars, Messieurs the Arch-deacons, Deacons, and Sub-deacons, Messieurs the Prebendaries, Messieurs the Churchwardens, Messieurs the Sextons, Messieurs the Beadles, Messieurs the Church-door-openers, and the "religious" men, as they say. Yes, we admit, without hesitation, M. Bonaparte had for him all those bishops who cross themselves like Veuillot and Montalembert, and all those religious men, a priceless, ancient race, but largely increased and recruited since the landholders' terrors of 1848, who pray in this wise: "O, my God! send up the Lyons shares! Dear Lord Jesus, see to it that I make a profit of twenty-five per cent, on my Rothschild-Neapolitan bonds! Holy Apostles, sell my wines for me! Blessed Martyrs, double my rents!"[10]

In the years of the Third Republic (1870–1940), the French general Georges Boulanger as minister of war quickly became a celebrity by denouncing the sordid market for military decorations. He was soon the most popular man in the country. He went into politics and founded a movement of his own. But his adventure in politics was meteoric and his rocketing career ended as quickly as it had begun. The general was accused of plotting a coup d'état and he died as a suicide in exile. It was also in France in the second half of the century that the growing indebtedness of the state became a source of great concern. The factors at play were risky undertakings in the realm of foreign policy and the management of public finance that left so much margin for personal discretion and corruption that even Napoleon III was induced to transfer certain of his fiscal powers to the French parliament.

In this atmosphere, in 1889, the Panama Canal Scandal exploded. Ferdinand de Lesseps, who had been one of the key figures behind the construction of the Suez Canal, launched a massive promotional campaign to promote and finance his new undertaking. It has been written that he handed out more than 4 million francs in the currency of the time to the press and to politicians to induce them to pass laws favorable to the project. When the company went bankrupt, thousands of small investors were ruined, but the true culprits, who enjoyed powerful political protection, were not prosecuted. The scandal ended in 1893 when the case was archived, causing a groundswell of public indignation.

In the meantime, in the recently and not easily unified Italy, Agostino Depretis was inaugurating a new political experiment that would go down in Italian history under the name *trasformismo*: a political system based on the systematic changing of the guard of majorities, a method that according to the views of most historians would rapidly facilitate the spread of government corruption, both on a state level and in the outlying administrations. Mario Pacelli, a professor of law and a scholar of Italian history, wrote that with "Garibaldi, Mazzini, Cavour, Gioberti, Ricasoli, Minghetti: the list of the 'fathers' of the homeland could continue at length. Official rhetoric has often described them as individuals concerned only with the public good. . . . Too good to be true: and in fact it wasn't true. Alongside the official Italy dripping with public virtue, there exists another permeated with public and private

vices, corruption, vexations large and small, and carefully concealed truths."[11] As early as 1865, Massimo
d'Azeglio wrote in a letter to his wife, "If you only knew
what a conspiracy of frauds and schemers now extends
over Italy, you'd be afraid as I am."[12]

Those were the years in which the right held power
and the same years that witnessed the development of the
notorious scandal of the *monopolio dei tabacchi*, the
state tobacco monopoly. Between 1868 and 1869 Italy's
prime minister was Luigi Menabrea, who in a challenging
economic situation made an effort to reduce the public
debt. Faced with the unwillingness of Italian and foreign
bankers to provide massive injections of credit, he was
"obliged" not only to impose an odious tax on milled
wheat and other grains and cereals but also to subcon-
tract to third parties the state monopoly on tobacco. The
mastermind of the episode was Domenico Balduino,
managing director of Credito Mobiliare. For twenty years
a limited-liability company would manage the monopoly
and pay the Italian state 180 million lire in gold. The
suspicions that the operation would eventually procure
for both politicians and middlemen a percentage on the
deal arose immediately and were probably well founded.
It was said that even King Victor Emmanuel II was the
potential recipient of a bribe of 6 million lire in the money
of the time. It is almost certain that no less than 50 million of the 180 million paid by the subcontractors wound
up in private pockets instead of the state coffers. But amid
a succession of parliamentary imbroglios, the mysterious
wounding of a member of parliament, and journalistic investigations, the scandal vanished into thin air, and had
the sole effect of contributing to the fall of the Menabrea

government. There are few who now remember that the wounded parliamentarian was Cristiano Lobbia, a member for Asiago, one of the most fervent accusers in the tobacco scandal. If his name has gone down in history in Italy, it has nothing to do with the staunch position the left-wing member of parliament took for the liberal party, but is rather because of the hat he wore. He was the target of an attack in Florence, where the parliament of the Kingdom of Italy was still located, and was clubbed and stabbed. He survived the attack, but afterwards his hat had a dent in the middle. Thanks to the commercial initiative of an enterprising Milanese hat maker, his name came to be used for a style of hat with a crease in the center of the crown and the brim turned up all around, the Lobbia. In spite of this everlasting fame, the bribe maneuver with all the connivances and intrigues it carried with it remained unpunished.

Another scandal involved the Italian railroads. The zoning plans of the cities and territories of Italy that were involved in the development of the railway network were cunningly maneuvered so as to profit a group of powerful financiers, aristocratic landowners, politicians, and cardinals led by Pietro Bastogi, who, in 1862, as minister of finance, sold the southern Italian railways to a private company—keeping for himself a chunk of cash worth 14 million lire in the currency of the time. But the greatest scandal of all was that of the Banca Romana, founded in 1835 with Belgian and French capital. In 1893 it was involved in a criminal trial that dragged in many of its officers and several members of the government, presided over by Giovanni Giolitti. At the center of the affair was the figure of Bernardo Tanlongo, an unscrupulous profiteer who had found a very handy way to promote his own career and win favors for the bank he ran, issuing bills of exchange and distributing bribes to a group of profiteers and politicians.

Francesco Crispi was the first to make use of Tanlongo's favors, taking payments amounting to roughly a million euros in today's money; he then attempted to undermine Giolitti's legitimacy, in a clumsy attempt to bring down his government. However, Crispi was the one who emerged bruised and beaten, because Giolitti showed no hesitation in revealing the truth about Crispi, as well as discrediting Crispi's private conduct. In those same years, Luigi Pirandello wrote, in *The Old and the Young,*

> Why yes, indeed: the skies of Italy, in these days, were raining down mud, and people were rolling it into balls and throwing them; and the mud was sticking everywhere, on the pale, distorted faces of assailed and assailants, on the medals won in the past on fields of battle (these, at least, ought surely to have been held sacred!) and on crosses and orders and gold-laced coats and on the door-plates of Government and newspaper offices. It rained torrents of mud; and it seemed as though all the sewers of the city had overflowed, and the new national existence of the third Rome must be swamped in that turbid, fetid flood of mire, over which hovered screaming—black birds of prey— calumny and suspicion.[13]

In late nineteenth-century Italy the relationships of patronage that lay behind the election of a member of parliament guaranteed for better or worse the representation of certain questions emerging from society that would otherwise remain unanswered. The Notable, a key figure in the politics of those decades, ensured his support of the aspiring member of parliament in exchange for favors on behalf of his clientele.

It was at the end of the nineteenth century that Felice Cavallotti wrote these lines: "In less pleasant, more ferocious days / thieves were strung up on crosses. / In less ferocious, more pleasant days / crosses are strung around the necks of thieves."[14] In 1895, in fact, the prime minister of Italy, Francesco Crispi, was accused by Felice Cavallotti, a member of parliament, of having obtained illegal compensation for the attribution of a high honorific—the medal of the Order of Saints Maurice and Lazarus—to the profiteer Cornelio Hertz. Although the accusation would seem to be relatively venial, it was at the center of a harsh parliamentary polemic and the vehement "Letter to Honest Men of All Parties" by Cavallotti, which at the time caused a certain amount of outrage. With arguments not entirely unlike those used today by politicians who are caught in flagrante delicto as they give in to the widespread practice of malfeasance, Crispi tried to show that the fifty thousand lire paid to him represented a fee for professional services that had been performed some time earlier.

Francesco De Sanctis, who was a member of parliament in the Kingdom of Italy and who numerous times held the cabinet post of minister of public instruction—and wrote a memorable journal of one of his campaign tours throughout the length of the Italian peninsula—made a distinction in his *History of Italian Literature* between the phenomena *corruttela*, or depravity, and *corruzione*, or corruption. The first, De Sanctis explains, appears as a sort of "meta-sin," or "meta-crime," and that is a "generic disposition to the ineluctability of fraud." The latter, the more concrete and direct form of corruption, was in a certain sense illustrated in 1881 by the leader of the Italian Destra Storica, or Historical Right, Marco Minghetti, who published a study titled *The Political Parties and Their Interference in Justice and Administration*, an outright *j'accuse* before its time of the rule of political parties, or "particracy," and the tentacles it extends into the realm of the administration of justice. It focused on the misdeeds that the so-called government of liberal notables were engaging in, even back then, tending to "favor their friends and oppress their adversaries."

And yet even in this corrupt milieu there was no shortage of exceptions—which, as we well know, prove the rule. The Italian patriot Benedetto Cairoli was famously a man of great rectitude and was proud to be known as such. When he was a cabinet minister, he paid for his own carriage and for diplomatic meals, to such an extent that he took his own family up to and over the brink of utter ruin. But clearly, his was an isolated case in Italy, and in the rest of Europe, things weren't much better. William Gladstone's decision to attack Egypt in 1882 may well have had as much to do with worries over the national uprising in the country as with the fact that Gladstone himself had heavily invested in the Egyptian economy and by 1881 owned 51,000 pounds' worth of bonds, and the Suez Canal was of course crucial to the British economy, providing the indispensable connection to the empire's money chest, India. Conflict of interest, or at least the intersection of interests, was the driving force as never before.

It was the time of a crisis that spread throughout the Old World at the end of the nineteenth century and the beginning of the twentieth, the time of the end of empires. Now emerged decadent heroes who took hedonism and a snobbish detachment from "the gray deluge of democratic mud" as their very reason to live: characters such as Joris-Karl Huysmans's Jean Des Esseintes (1889), Oscar Wilde's Dorian Gray (1892), and Gabriele D'Annunzio's Andrea Sperelli, the protagonist of *The Child of Pleasure* (1889).[15] They were emblematic in the same sense as the young protagonist in the previously mentioned *The Shadowless Man; Or, The Wonderful History of Peter Schlemihl*, by Adelbert von Chamisso (1781–1838), in which Peter, in order to make his entrance into the comfortable and respectable world of the middle class and redeem himself from the poverty into which he was born, is ready to sell his own shadow in exchange for Fortunatus's bottomless purse. Too late, he realizes the Faustian error he has made. As Chamisso points out, "The science of finance instructs us sufficiently respecting the value of money; the value of a shadow is less generally acknowledged. My thoughtless friend was covetous of money, of which he knew the value, and forgot to think upon solid substance."[16]

The price of such a rapid expansion, of such wide-ranging and endemic corruption, and of such an unreasonable faith in social climbing at all and any costs was about to be paid. The shadow that was now starting to loom over Europe was of a bloodbath about to be unleashed.

As Mario Silvestri writes in *Decadenza dell'Europa occidentale 1890–1946*, "The First World War (even more than the Second) appears as a destructive event of an irreversible nature, a veritable explosion that uprooted the existing political, economic, social, and military equilibriums, which could not thereafter be restored. After that . . . Western Europe began to decline both materially and morally."[17]

TEN PARTS IN THE PLAY

*Corruption in the Depictions of the
Nineteenth-Century Novel*

NINETEENTH-CENTURY LITERATURE gave us unforgettable figures of the corrupted and the corrupters which not only
offer us a particularly piercing gaze into the society of the
times and its profiteers, but also crystallize archetypes
that have taken on their own existence. One of the most
long-lived of these archetypes is also one of the customary faces of corruption in the literature of the nineteenth
century: the professional journalist. This figure continued to appear in novels and other fiction and later, in
films. Think of the scoundrel character Bel Ami in Guy de
Maupassant's novel of the same name, who, thanks to the
allure he exercises over the women who adore him, climbs
rung after rung on the social ladder, progressing from
journalism to politics and, finally, to finance. Or, in a

lighter vein, think of George Flack, the remorseless hack created by Henry James—who admired Maupassant's *Bel Ami*—who does not hesitate to endanger a friend's love affair in order to boost sales of the scandal sheet he works for, *The Reverberator*, also the story's title. "I try to get the people what they want. It's hard work," says Flack of his job.[1] And the sentence rings true because it is one of the widest-spread justifications for corruption. Together with "everybody does it," of course.

Alongside the journalist, and partially overlapping him, is the swindler. "Then Madame Caroline acquired the sudden conviction," we read in a novel by Émile Zola, *L'argent* (Money),

> that money was the dungheap in which grew the humanity of tomorrow. . . . If her brother over yonder in the East was in such high spirits, shouting victory amidst the workshops and yards which were being got in order, and the buildings which were springing from the soil, it was because the passion for gambling was making money rain down and rot everything in Paris. Poisonous and destructive money became the ferment of all social vegetation, served as the necessary compost for the execution of the great works which would draw the nations nearer together and pacify the earth. She had cursed money, and now she fell in awe-stricken admiration before it.[2]

The protagonist of Zola's novel is Saccard, a con man of the first order who arrives in Paris determined to take his revenge for the misadventures suffered in the past. He immediately conquers the Bourse (the stock market) by founding no less than a universal bank, and he wins over men and women through his promises that he will expand his business to the West and Far East. Madame Caroline is one of the characters who gives in to the swindler's charm, until the inevitable bankruptcy that will sweep over Saccard at the end of the story.

There is no happy ending either for Alphonse Daudet's *Le Nabab* (The nabob), set in Paris in the second half of the nineteenth century. In this book an Irish doctor and charlatan is surrounded by an authentic circus of beggars and thieves, penniless adventurers, poor office clerks, bankers, and rich profiteers such as Jansoulet (the nabob of the title), who, thanks to his wide variety of speculations and business deals, becomes a multimillionaire in Tunis. A contrived network of disparate interests ultimately collapses of its own weight: Jansoulet's election to parliament goes up in smoke, and so does most of his wealth and even his marriage.

Zola's *The Fortune of the Rougons* is another in a long succession of portraits of the era that denounces the moral and political degeneracy of the Second Empire. Published in 1871, it is the first book of the twenty-novel Rougon-Macquart cycle conceived by Zola with the intention of illustrating the history of France of his time through the story and experiences of a single family.[3] At the center of the tale, in a provincial setting characterized by the pursuit of power and the lust for prestige and wealth, is the hatred between two branches of a single family: the Rougons are the legitimate branch and the Macquarts are a money-hungry bastard branch. The story turns even harsher with the outbreak of the revolution of 1848. The novel reveals, through the events leading up to the birth of the Second Empire, the author's struggle to portray the transition, violent at times, from agrarian wealth to the petty and grand bourgeoisie of "business affairs."

The dilemma, both ethical and metaphysical, of individual responsibility emerges with incomparable dramatic force from Dostoyevsky's portrait of czarist Russia of the late nineteenth-century that we find in his novels. His Christian roots led him to that timeless torment of doubt that suffuses the pages of *Brothers Karamazov*, including Ivan's famous provocation: If there is no immortal soul, no virtue can possibly exist, and therefore everything is permitted. And if man is tragically free, as we also read in "Environment," from *A Writer's Diary*, a collection of pieces Dostoyevsky wrote for a newspaper, we will eventually come to the conclusion that crimes do not exist at all and we should blame it all on the environment.

But it is perhaps in the English-language fiction that we find one of the strongest expressions of social protest in the literature of the time. That's certainly understandable in a period of troubled transformation in England, characterized by the great poverty that industrialization had brought to the weakest classes. Anthony Trollope, the son of a lawyer, witnessed his own family's ruin before finding a position in the General Post Office and a certain fortune in the prolific composition of novels. Victorian society and its vices were the authentic protagonists of his many novels, from *The Warden* to *Phineas Finn*. The latter novel features an ambitious young man who becomes a member of parliament by easily winning over the favors of his district, where the "inhabitants were so far removed from the world, and were so ignorant of the world's good things, that they knew nothing about bribery."[4] And yet when Trollope himself ran as a candidate for parliament, he was beaten by a conservative opponent who might have been better than him or might have been more versed in the art of giving the voters what they wanted, that is, cash on the nail. Trollope described the experience in *The Prime Minister* and in *The Duke's Children*, where, in the imaginary electoral district of Silverbridge, the votes of the citizenry can be bought for the best offer.

The decline of the Victorian era would be extensively satirized by George Bernard Shaw, and dramatically portrayed in a novelistic cycle in John Galsworthy's *The Forsyte Saga*. The latter is a classic panorama of the customs of a cross section of English society, as told through the story of a family of the upper middle classes, beginning in the Victorian era. The first novel of the saga, *The Man of Property*, has among its protagonists the founder of the Forsyte family's prosperity in the times of England's great commercial expansion. But the true representative of the Forsyte mindset is his son: a man of property willing to compromise everything in order to further the family's fortune.

The writer H. G. Wells is said to have commented about the profiteer Max Aitken, the first Baron Beaverbrook, of Fleet Street, "If Max ever gets to Heaven, he won't last long." Beaverbrook had been accused of a serious stock fraud when he had basically managed to corner the market on cement in Canada, and it was the making of his fortune.[5] "He will be chucked out for trying to pull off a merger between Heaven and Hell after having secured a controlling interest in key subsidiary companies in both places of course," was Wells's prediction. Beaverbrook was the target of Evelyn Waugh's irony as well, and was portrayed in Waugh's novel *Scoop* as Lord Copper.

The Scottish philosopher and historian Thomas Carlyle (1795–1881), who believed in a history of heroes and the existence of a "genius of history," acknowledged that in some eras payment in cash is the only relationship between individuals. And this "harsh law" proved itself true in the search for political consensus described in Charles Dickens's savory satire *The Pickwick Papers*. In the quaint little town of Eatanswill the protagonists of the story find themselves in the midst of an election campaign in full swing, an exemplary battle, no holds barred, between the "buff" and the "blue":

> During the whole time of the polling, the town was in a perpetual fever of excitement. Everything was conducted on the most liberal and delightful scale. Excisable articles were remarkably cheap at all the public-houses; and spring vans paraded the streets for the accommodation of voters who were seized with any temporary dizziness in the head—an epidemic which prevailed among the electors, during the contest, to a most alarming extent, and under the influence of which they might frequently be seen lying on the pavements in a state of utter insensibility. A small body of electors remained unpolled on the very last day. They were calculating and reflecting persons, who had not yet been convinced by the arguments of either party, although they had frequent conferences with each. One hour before the close of the poll,

Mr. Perker solicited the honour of a private interview with these intelligent, these noble, these patriotic men. It was granted. His arguments were brief but satisfactory. They went in a body to the poll; and when they returned, the Honourable Samuel Slumkey, of Slumkey Hall, was returned also.[6]

In reality, as Lewis Carroll so brilliantly shows in *Alice's Adventures in Wonderland*, each of the participants in the caucus race proposed by the Dodo on the shore of the lake of tears is a winner and must have a prize, although they've done nothing but run in a circle, "the best thing to get us dry."

The prize, in short, is not the election but access to the benefices that politics knows how to proffer generously, often to the losers. The poet and Pre-Raphaelite painter William Morris wrote, in *News from Nowhere*: "The parties . . . only *pretended* to this serious difference of opinion; for if it had existed they could not have dealt together in the ordinary business of life; couldn't have eaten together, bought and sold together, gambled together, cheated other people together." In reference to the transformation of parliament into a sort of dung market Morris observed: "Well, well, dung is not the worst kind of corruption; fertility may come of that, whereas mere dearth came from the other kind, of which those walls once held the great supporters."[7]

In the London of the late nineteenth and early twentieth centuries we encounter another rather typical corruptor and swindler, the English politician and financier Horatio Bottomley, well known for having founded the *Financial Times*, but also for having elevated the con game to an art form, although he still managed to get himself thrown into a jail cell in 1922. This is how he was described in *The New Statesman* (June 3, 1922): "He possessed that sort of genius that repeatedly drew our eyes from the victims." In the face of such stunning shamelessness, the newspaper admitted, even one's moral sense might have experienced a sort of suspension.

Separating vice from virtue, in other words, would seem to be a game destined ultimately to shatter against the hard surface of a reality that is far more complex than we choose to depict it. Let us take the American president Abraham Lincoln: he was an outstanding statesman, but he was also convinced, like so many others, that in politics one cannot be exempted from making use of all means necessary to attain one's end. This was because to him, on some issues success was a moral duty. In fact, during the struggle to pass the Thirteenth Amendment to the U. S. Constitution, to abolish slavery, which required a two-thirds vote of Congress, the president had no doubts: since only two votes were lacking to secure approval of the amendment, he explained that those two votes must be obtained at any cost: "Those two votes must be procured. I leave it to you to determine how it shall be done; but remember that I am President of the United States, clothed with immense power, and I expect you to procure those votes."[8] It was a foregone conclusion: The Constitution was in fact amended, and slavery was abolished once and for all.

Let us return to Europe, however, where at the century's end, the moral issues that echo through the nineteenth-century stories of the rise and fall of swindlers are undermined by a general paradigm shift, that of course also affects the literary depiction of corruption. In the Vienna of the early twentieth century, the journalist Karl Kraus (1874–1936) was an implacable persecutor of the spreading corruption—so successful that he was able to chase the notorious profiteer Bekessy out of the Austrian capital. In *The Last Days of Mankind* Kraus wrote, "Day after day it was a reign marked by intellectual decline, casual neglect and corruption of the noblest national characteristics unparalleled in world history."[9] In the same years and city as Kraus, Sigmund Freud, the father of psychoanalysis, contributed indelibly to the mythology of the link between manure and money, though without dissuading the ranks of monotheistic worshippers of money. Freud noted that society treats money with the same hypocrisy with which it treats sex, being in denial about the true nature of both: acquiring power over people. But wealth, by turning a man into an alchemist, ultimately destines him to self-destruction, as happened with King Midas.

For that matter, in every country and time "the abuse and disobedience of the law cannot be prevented by any law," a disheartened Giacomo Leopardi wrote in his *Discourse on the Present State of the Customs of the Italians*.[10] But even more clearly, "It is clear from the aforesaid things that Italy is, as far as morality is concerned, less provided with foundations than perhaps any other civil European nation." It is the country of courtiers, condemned by Verdi's Rigoletto as an "accursed race of courtiers." Ugo Foscolo admitted perhaps more prosaically that "as long as one lives in a society where money is the representative of all life's needs and comforts, and is moreover the tool of individual independence, one cannot hold it in contempt unless one is either divinely exempt from all need or stol-idly indifferent to one's independence."[11]

In Italy, too, a country where a tendency to political corruption reemerged in the nineteenth century—perhaps amplified by the recent unification—novelists have given us unforgettable characters. Carlino, the protagonist of Ippolito Nievo's *Confessions of an Italian*, even though he is living through a particularly stormy period of the country's history (from the Napoleonic campaigns to the uprisings of 1848), seems determined to give the lie to the cliché of the average Italian who is always ready to compromise. The grandson of the Count of Fratta, Car-lino invites us to use a "shield against the seductions of false friends, the deceit of the vile and the abuse of the powerful."[12]

But behind every "virtuous" Carlino we can find a far less edifying Mastro Don Gesualdo, protagonist and ep-onym of the second novel in the cycle of *I vinti* (The los-ers) by Giovanni Verga, and a perfect incarnation of the figure of the parvenu. Having progressed from the status of a bricklayer eager to foment a "revolution" to that of prosperous landowner determined to safeguard his inter-ests against all possible social change, Gesualdo Motta is a grasping opportunist who has sacrificed any and all real passion to *la roba*, his possessions, shedding true affec-tion in favor of profit, and thus condemning himself to an empty, lonely death.

In Federico De Roberto's *The Viceroys* (1894), the Duke of Oragua, untroubled by doubts, states, "Now that we have made Italy, we must mind our own business."[13] This is the Italy that begins with the Risorgimento, the process of unification so roundly criticized these days, a country where, as Angelo Panebianco points out, Cavour himself said "that if he had committed for purposes of personal self-interest even just a tiny part of what he had done in order to bring about the unification of Italy, he would rightly be considered among the worst evildoers imaginable."[14] But corruption concerns history writ large every bit as much as it does history on a more minute, everyday scale. When we read *Le miserie di Monsù Travet* by Vittorio Bersezio or the satire, *Messieurs les ronds-de-cuir*, by the French author Georges Courteline, we find clearly stated that only cunning can help us find a way in the swamp of public administration; cunning, and the oiling of bureaucracy's rusty mechanisms. And this also seems to hold at higher levels. "You may have been told that nowadays an election costs money," we read in *The Viceroys*, "but remember what Mugnòs wrote about the Viceroy Lopez Ximenes, who had to offer thirty thousand *scudi* to King Ferdinand in order to keep his job."[15]

Among the many stories that seem to foreshadow the frauds and swindles of the present day—and not only in Italy—there is, of course, *The Adventures of Pinocchio* (1883) by Carlo Collodi. The protagonist of the book, having buried his few coins in the Field of Miracles on the advice of the Cat and the Fox, returns to the site of the hole, wondering how many thousands of coins he's likely to find on the tree that will have grown where he planted his coins, "invested" with such blind faith. Alas, the two villains have returned to dig up the coins and abscond with them. On hearing Pinocchio's tale of the robbery, the judge declares, " 'This poor simpleton has been robbed of four gold pieces. Take him, therefore, and throw him into prison.' The Marionette, on hearing this sentence passed upon him, was thoroughly stunned. He tried to protest, but the two officers clapped their paws on his mouth and hustled him away to jail."[16]

The crime committed by Geppetto's creation is unmistakable: in the lands of successful cats and foxes, he made the unforgivable mistake of allowing himself to be robbed.

ELEVEN THE GREAT DICTATORSHIPS

Totalitarian Corruption in the First Half of the Twentieth Century

THE TRAUMA AND THE SORROWS of the First World War, along with the intense discontent of the working masses struggling with the twin evils of poverty and an economic downturn and the demands of the growing veterans' movements, inevitably produced a powerful widespread state of social malaise that largely translated into an intolerance of the ruling class then in power (in many cases, the same people as before the war) and a growing predisposition toward extremist political movements on both the right and the left. In the France of the early 1930s, shaken by a grave inflationary crisis, there was an explosive financial scandal linked to the name of Serge-Alexandre Stavisky, immortalized as a great swindler in the film *Stavisky*, with Jean-Paul Belmondo in the title

role. Stavisky was a Ukrainian emigré capable of invent-
ing a bank out of whole cloth and defrauding thousands
of French citizens—he had tried the same exploit in the
midst of the First World War, with the Germans at the
gates—only to shuffle off the public stage in a rather mysterious manner in 1934. The scandal presented the opportunity that the right wing was waiting for to charge the
government with corruption and rock Paris with grave
public disorders. In Europe, these were the years in which
extremist movements were established or consolidated,
movements that paid lip service to a denunciation of the
old parties inured to compromise and exhausted from an
opaque management of power, only to fall into the same
vices that they'd so passionately denounced the minute
the tables were turned and they had seized the levers of
power themselves, either through elections of coups d'état.

The great dictatorships of the twentieth century, without exception, rose to power by promising change and
reform, by encouraging a new order of honesty. And
without exception they proceeded to elevate corruption
to an art of governing. In the Third Reich, Reich Marshal
Hermann Göring accumulated enormous wealth through
his position of power and, in particular, thanks to the
brutal plunder that followed the occupation of enemy nations. In the years of the Third Reich, men like Rudolf
Hess, Joseph Goebbels, Heinrich Himmler, and countless
other officers and courtiers of Hitler's inner circle enriched themselves, exploiting their power and privileges
while being members of a political party that took "purity" as its watchword and boasted of its fight against
greed and pettiness, which were of course touted as characteristics typical of Jews, as if that were one of its guiding

principles. A poster that summoned the crowds to one of Hitler's first public speeches, on May 11, 1920, read: "Citizens! Do not believe that the Germany of misfortune and misery, the nation of corruption and usury, the land of Jewish corruption, can be saved by parties that claim to stand on a foundation of facts. Never!" And yet, in spite of the strictures of censorship and Hitlerian propaganda that so effectively silenced scandals and claims of malfeasance, a 1935 Berlin police report states: "It is with bitterness that we observe on all sides that the very functionaries of the Party lead quite scandalous lives, devoting themselves to gluttony, plunder, and malfeasance and cultivating a decadent attitude reminiscent of the times prior to the war."[1] Starting with the Night of the Long Knives (when the S.S. set upon the S.A., hurling at the S.A. chief, Ernst Roehm, as a justification for his murder, the accusation of sexual perversion, among others), and with increasing ferocity as the war progressed, accusations of economic, sexual, and political corruption constituted a customary weapon in the fights that pitted the various factions of the Nazi hierarchies against each other—brown shirts and black shirts, S.D. and S.S. It was all encouraged by the Fuehrer's growing paranoia.

On April 29, 1938, about a month after the Anschluss of Austria, Reichsfuehrer-SS Heinrich Himmler and a number of other ranking SS officers founded in Berlin the Deutsche Erd- und Steinwerke GmbH (German Earth and Stone Works Company, Inc.), known as DEST, with capital of 10,000 marks. They immediately received a deposit of 9.5 million marks, an interest-free mortgage made by the General Building Inspectorate, headed by Albert Speer, and had plans to begin construction of a concentration camp in the township of Mauthausen, near Linz. But before they started work on the camp itself they had to solve the problem of purchasing the stone quarries present within the boundaries of the township. One of the quarries was owned by the city of Vienna. DEST offered an annual rent of 5,000 marks, a share in the profits, and supplies of raw materials. Hitler and Speer already had major architectural projects in mind for Berlin and other cities, and Theodor Eicke, the commandant of Dachau, began to design a camp whose prisoners "would produce materials for the construction of buildings for the Reich" by working the quarries around Mauthausen. Even in Nazi Austria, though, the assigning of public works contracts took time, and the Viennese administration remained unpersuaded. In the quarry there was very fine material to be extracted, according to the experts in the various commissions with jurisdiction over the matter, and not only did that material rightly belong to the city which has need of it, but quarrying it required trained personnel, not forced laborers with no prior experience. It was the mayor of Vienna who cut the discussion short, supporting the point of view of the S.S. and pushing his administration to accept the offer. Work in the quarries under the new management began in May 1938, with the first political prisoners also constructing the camp. In the meantime, DEST received further financing of 8 million marks from the German Red Cross, whose finances were being managed by another S.S. officer, Oswald Pohl, in his role as head of the Verwaltungsamtes-SS, the SS administration, which administered the whole concentration camp system. DEST signed a contract to supply building materials to Speer's General Building Inspectorate.

There wasn't the slightest hint of free market dynamics, while there was plenty of evidence of back scratching and trading favors. No question, there was plenty of profit: In 1942 the quarries of Mauthausen invoiced 1,552,000 marks; 3,800,100 marks in 1943; and 11,029,000 marks in 1944.

Hannah Arendt, a scholar of totalitarianism who coined the term "banality of evil"—and of the failure of all ethics based upon obedience to the law, as in the paradigmatic case of Adolf Eichmann—points out that for these regimes, the utilitarian aspects were not essential because what the regimes were aiming at was infinitely more ambitious: the transformation of reality so that it matches the suppositions of the dominant ideology. She makes a distinction between full-fledged totalitarian regimes, like those under Hitler and Stalin, and authoritarian regimes like that of Mussolini.

Theoretical distinctions aside, there is in any case no doubt that illicit profit taking, encouraged by the privileges afforded to the few, were a constant under both Hitler and Stalin, and under Mussolini and Franco, too. Even Spanish neutrality in the Second World War (which was anything but absolute, since a division of volunteers fought in the Soviet Union) was probably a position purchased at a very dear price by Churchill and the Allies. Information has come to light on the role played by the banker Juan March as an effective middleman for relations with the British. Franco, of course, was an enemy of the republican parties, which were accused of being among the leading causes of Spanish decadence and the protagonists of numerous scandals such as the one denounced to the Cortes Generales, Spain's legislature, by the inspector general for the colonies, Antonio Nombela—it was just one of the many episodes that led to the disintegration of the radical republican party then leading the government. But Franco's regime inevitably wound up slipping into an even darker climate of corruption with the involvement of functionaries and officers of the regime; the bankruptcy of the steel mills of Madrid, involved Franco's brother. The autarkic policies of El Caudillo's regime, which certainly contributed to the impoverishment of Spain during the years of his dictatorship, included the organization of the black market under government control, with the systematic concession of illegal commercial licenses in exchange for payments.

During the same years, the Kingdom of Italy was also preparing to knuckle under to a dictatorship. An analysis of the contributing factors can be found in the writings of Antonio Gramsci, who blames the inherent weakness of the democratic nature of the state that emerged from the Risorgimento—the absence of any real popular and national unity—and the inefficacy of actions taken by liberal governments incapable of facing up with any adequate measures to the complex social and economic situation inherited after the First World War (irredentism, the formation of mass political parties, union activism). The most important factor, though, was the failure to understand the subversive nature of Fascism, in which so many placed hopes for a definitive return to order and stability. "What comes to pass does so not so much because a few people want it to happen, as because the mass of citizens abdicate their responsibility and let things be," Gramsci pointed out, "but few people, if any, see their indifference as a fault—their scepticism, their failure to give moral and material support to those political and economic groups that were struggling either to avoid a particular evil or to promote a particular good."[2]

Piero Gobetti, who died after a savage beating by the Fascists, also insisted on this national shortcoming: "We fought Mussolini the corruptor before Mussolini the tyrant; we fought fascism as paternal tutelage before fascism as a dictatorship; we did not insist on complaining about the lack of liberty and about violence, but turned our attention to our polemic with the Italians, those who did not put up resistance, that allowed themselves to be tamed."[3] As Leo Longanesi suggested, the nation's flag ought to be emblazoned with the motto *Tengo famiglia* (I have a family).[4] The Italians defended themselves from a sinful and hostile state with friendships, favors, compromises, alliances, and family ties, which made it possible to sidestep obstacles, leapfrog regulations, and in any case always obtain by any means possible the permit, the license, or the favor considered indispensable because taking care of the family was all-important.

There were many cases of corruption during the Fascist period: from Galeazzo Ciano and his wife, Edda, daughter of Il Duce, all the way up to Renato Ricci, the head of the Opera Nazionale Balilla Fascist youth movement, who was doing land-office business thanks to the marble quarries in his hometown, Carrara. Although from the very outset of the dictatorship Fascism got its beginnings denouncing the corruption of mores in parliamentary democracy and its protagonists, as was predictable the moralistic phase of the movement soon gave way to the more predatory phase. The murder of the member of parliament Giacomo Matteotti in 1924 came hard on

the heels of his denunciatory speeches in the Italian parliament, in particular, his charges concerning economic
abuses, favors, piloted contracts, and illicit profits. Among
other things, Matteotti had denounced serious irregularities
on the part of the Finance Ministry concerning sugar im-
ports, which were particularly expensive to Italian con-
sumers and which made the sugar merchants rich (it is
well known just how generous that industry was in its financing of the Fascists in their early years). Matteotti had
also called into question the contract for the construction
of two major rail lines at a cost of a billion lire in the currency of the time, which had been given to contractors
who were close to the government and to a company that
had direct ties to a member of the Public Works Council.

But this was only the beginning of the Fascist era.
Later on, everything would go smoothly, without hindrance
of any kind. One well-known instance of corruption in
high office is the case of the *gerarca* (Fascist Party official)
of Cremona, Roberto Farinacci, who as a lawyer made
use of his political influence without any qualms to win
his cases and recruit new clients. "His Excellency Farinacci," it was noted in reports made to Il Duce, "has created for himself such wealth that he is able to wallow in
the most refined luxuries in very expensive hotels."[5] He
also had very particular tastes when it came to sex, tastes
that are reminiscent of more recent Italian heads of state:
"He brought to his apartment, among others, the coed
philosophy student A.R., a virgin. Apparently he wants
these girls, some of them underage, in the uniforms of the
Young Italian Girls Movement."[6] Another high party official, Italo Balbo, renamed a section of land that in time
became famous as Punta Ala, had a provincial road built

there that to all intents and purposes was private, and equipped his estate with all possible comforts at the expense of the public purse.

It is somewhat symbolic, if not particularly original that Fascism ended with Il Duce's attempt to flee and to take the loot of the Italian Social Republic with him—something like 100 million lire of the time, according to some sources, and with the mystery bound up with the disappearance of the "treasure of Dongo" (the money, gold, and valuable artifacts) after the execution of Mussolini in the Swiss town of Dongo and the displaying of his corpse before the crowds in Piazzale Loreto in Milan.

The long centuries of servitude and tyranny experienced by Italy, as Piero Calamandrei wrote, were compounded by the "corruption of Fascist officials exercising their free right to engage in misappropriation and malfeasance."[7] Corruption was transformed into a "physiological tool of government," reinforced by the "extortionate complicity established among the various officials." It was a historical aspect of such importance that it led the historian Massimo Salvadori and the constitutional scholar Alessandro Pizzorusso to affirm that, while the transition from free-market liberalism to Fascism certainly constituted a sharp break, in terms of corruption the impression is that of a substantial continuity largely insured by the continued employment of the old bureaucratic staff and the civil servants of the public administration. Mussolini himself wrote in his preface to an edition of *The Prince*: "I believe Machiavelli's *The Prince* to be the statesman's supreme guide. His doctrine is alive today because in the course of four hundred years no deep changes have occurred in the minds of men." Curiously, as noted by the journalist Filippo Ceccarelli, both Bettino Craxi and Silvio Berlusconi wrote introductions to new editions of *The Prince*; Berlusconi even republished the book in his own publishing house. The Bolshevik Lev Kamenev also ordered the publication of a Russian translation of the Florentine author, and it is no secret that the Nazis considered the writings of the Florentine secretary Machiavelli to be a major point of reference.

Leaving aside all matters of Machiavellian inspiration, in any case, the picture painted by Marshal of Italy Pietro Badoglio (1871–1956) of the state of a country that had survived two decades of Fascist rule is perhaps more realistic and effective than any other subsequent historical reconstruction. "Fascism fell, not due to any external force, but because of an internal crisis," stated the marshal of Italy in a speech to his officers in the aftermath of the fall of the regime and the signing of the armistice, in his new responsibility as head of state. "I will not tell you everything that I have been able to see in this brief period running the government. But I will tell you a few outstanding facts. Agip, which you know very well: that famous oil company, a paragovernmental institution, had a deficit of 90 million lire, and we were unable to even lay hands on any accounting documents. GIL [Gioventù Italiana del Littorio, or Italian Youth of the Lictor, the consolidated youth movement of the National Fascist Party] cost the Italian state 1.7 billion lire. OND [Opera Nazionale del Dopolavoro, the National Recreational Club, the party's leisure and recreational organization for adults], 1.2 billion lire. The Ministry of Popular Culture had become a veritable bordello: It employed a vast number of Roman ladies on salaries that in some cases ranged from

8,000 to 10,000 lire monthly, with responsibilities . . . that I shall leave to your imaginations. . . . And that is why we were sent to war carrying rifles from 1891."[8]

We should add that the terrain from this point of view must have been quite fertile, given the fact that most historians agree that the advent of Fascism coincided with a progressive groundswell of corruption of the liberal national political system. But whereas in Giovanni Giolitti's administration (1901–1913), as Sergio Turone has pointed out, a kind of corruption settled in that tended to exclude the area of financial profits and outright bank fraud, the government still badly needed complicity with the outlying administrations (which would come in handy during elections), and through this channel dishonest notables and mayors acquired impunity for their acts of malfeasance. For Giolitti's inability to react to the system of clientelism, Gaetano Salvemini had dubbed him the "minister of the underworld." His unfortunate attempt to adhere to his favored political tactic of avoiding harsh conflict with his adversaries marked his progressive decline (he led his last government in 1920–1921) and that of the political system that had begun with the Risorgimento. In fact, the end of that system coincided with the aftermath of the Great War, and the advent of Mussolini as head of state.

Aldo Ravelli, one of the founding fathers of the Milan stock market, the *borsa*, testified that already in the 1930s the Guardia di Finanza, the financial police, was taking bribes throughout Italy. Not paying meant not working. But according to Ravelli the person who took the money, not the one who gave it, should go to prison. Corruption, it seems, united the country in spite of the extreme differences in development and living conditions between the north and the south of the peninsula.

In the twentieth century, the first socialist states also saw the light and established themselves with the intention of creating new societies where the corruption of free-market democracies was abolished. Unfortunately, those states were soon forced to face up to reality. The history of the Soviet Union reveals an inevitable system of payoffs and favor swapping that began at the lowest level of the kolkhozes and reached all the way up to the highest level of officialdom and government hierarchy in the administrative process (a system "assisted" to a not insignificant extent by the sheer vastness of the public machinery). The nomenklatura of the Soviet regime has always benefited from its role as a ruling caste: Its members have enjoyed the finest houses, separate facilities in every aspect of life, cars, and privileges of various sorts.

In *Animal Farm* (1944), George Orwell wrote an allegory of the Russian Revolution and its aftermath, although it is actually a satire of all absolutist utopias, destined as they are eventually to be transformed into totalitarian regimes. The story is that of the animals of Manor Farm, mistreated and exploited, who rise up in rebellion against their farmer, after being told of a dream that had come to Old Major, a wise old prize boar. The dream spoke of a time when the animals would regain their freedom. And so it seems to come to pass, at least at first: The animals change the name of the farm and give themselves a new set of commandments. But soon conflict breaks out and, as always, the law of the jungle prevails. In this case, the strongest are the boars, who begin trading with humans and in short order become increasingly corrupt, ultimately resume the old habits of the farmer, and break with the new rules. The commandments are changed reflecting utility, and the law stating that "all animals are equal" is soon given an additional clause, "but some animals are more equal than others." Old Major's dream has officially turned into a nightmare.

In *The Fifth Pestilence*, by the Russian author Aleksei Mikhailovich Remizov (1877–1957), the prosecutor Bobrov has been serving the law scrupulously for twenty years, and is the terror of lawbreakers throughout the region. But one day he begins to doubt his own profession and the judicial system of which he is a representative, starts drinking, and ultimately dies, cut down by an apoplectic fit. But he leaves behind a very revealing notebook in which he has listed the miseries of the land of Russia, the pogroms, the pointless violence of the police, the vast and widespread brigandage, the terrorism of the nihilists, the corruption of the judiciary, the abuses and wrongdoings visited by the upper classes upon the defenseless populace. In *The Little Golden Calf*, a satirical novel published in 1931, the Russian writers Ilya Ilf and Evgeny Petrov note bitterly, "The life of the country had changed over the course of the centuries, but the streets were still those of the legendary ages."[9] The story is about a swindler who, learning that in the period of the New Economic Policy (1917–1922) a minor clerk (the "little golden calf" of the title) has managed to set aside several million rubles, devises a plan to relieve him of his wealth. The plot device is actually a pretext for describing a journey through the country, focusing the reader's attention on the grotesque individuals and institutions who prosper there. The true central character is actually the

Russia of the years after the First World War and the Revolution, populated by parasites, profiteers, bureaucrats, and party leaders, all of them willing to stop at nothing.

Characters like this could be found in abundance earlier, in czarist Russia, for example, in Gogol's classic play, *The Government Inspector*, in which a minor functionary is mistaken by the inhabitants of a small town for an emissary from the central government. He is given, and accepts without turning a hair, all the gifts and cash offerings that are normally bestowed by local officials to persuade such a higher-up to turn a blind eye.

Despite the tradition of criminally corrupt activities in the history of both imperial Russia and the Soviet regime, its peak was almost certainly under Stalin, when the Great Terror, the purges, the political murders, and the deportations of dissidents affected equally politicians, intellectuals, members of the military, bureaucrats, and ordinary citizens who were "guilty" of wandering off the path of Moscow's orthodoxy. In such a time, the overall climate of abuse and threats could hardly help but encourage corruption at both the lowest and the most exalted levels. *The Master and Margarita*, by Mikhail Bulgakov (1891–1940), is unquestionably the most successful satire of a thoroughly rotten society. In its inimitably surreal style, the book denounces that country's nomenklatura, the corrupt and parasitic bureaucracy, the censorship, and the widespread custom of informing upon one and all. The person who advised Stalin to base the gulags on a foundation of a constant lack of food was an "exemplary" member of his court, Naftaly Frenkel, of whom Martin Amis writes, "It seems he had no ideology (he wanted only money and power), but in his literalism, his scientism, and his natural indifference to all human suffering Frenkel was an excellent Bolshevik."[10]

Few nations have fallen prey to a blind and absolute power the way the USSR did. In order to better understand the chilling outlines and sheer dimensions of the Soviet dictatorship, it was necessary to await the Khrushchev years and the process of "de-Stalinization." After that, especially in the aftermath of the Brezhnev interlude, we had to wait for the arrival of perestroika and glasnost, ushered in at the behest of Mikhail Gorbachev, before we could glimpse the results of a series of reforms intended to abolish the decadence and corruption concealed by years of propaganda by means of a process of economic modernization. After an initial burst of enthusiasm, however, the country's economic and political decline could not be halted. That's not all: After Gorbachev and Yeltsin, throughout the area of Communist nations, right up until the reunification of Germany in 1990 and the disintegration of the USSR after 1991, the very process of reconversion to capitalism brought about such chaotic turmoil that a general wave of corruption swept the country, and the new process of deregulation only amplified that wave, so that even today, in 2017, the results constitute a state of emergency.

In the former USSR there has been a drastic and generalized reduction in the standard of living and new scandals involving organized crime have ultimately taken the place of the oppression and abuses, the favoritisms and horrors of the old regime, fomenting new waves of discontent and even resuscitating a nostalgic yearning for the past that would have been unthinkable until recently. One of the largest scandals in Putin's Russia involved Yukos, the largest Russian company in the energy sector. Its top managers were arrested on charges of laundering money from criminal enterprises and helping to make almost $5 million dollars disappear, money that had been lent to Russia by the International Monetary Fund.

But, of course, totalitarianism is not limited to what happened in Europe in the thirties, or in eastern Europe, Asia, or southeast Asia. It is also about Central and South America, Fascist in nature, and in some cases Communist. In *Open Veins of Latin America* (1971) by the Uruguayan writer Eduardo Galeano summarizes the chronicle of hundreds of years of contradictions of a continent rich in resources and yet poor, exploited by foreign powers and humiliated by authoritarian regimes. Unsurprisingly the book was censored by the dictator Pinochet in Chile and the military dictatorship in Argentina.

In *The Autumn of the Patriarch*, Gabriel García Márquez portrays the perfect protagonist of any regime, where tyranny takes the form not only of repression at the highest political levels but also and no less crushingly of a wide net of petty personal acts of people with various types of power. Márquez's patriarch is the despotic dictator of a small Caribbean island. Violent, vindictive, and bloodthirsty, he lives in a palace that is in ruins, surrounded by postulants and adulators who cast a harsh light on the profound solitude of the most dissolute power.

Let us also consider the figure of "father of his country" in the Dominican Republic, Rafael Trujillo, whose fortune was summarized by Hans Magnus Enzensberger: "The figures reported by various biographers vary widely, ranging from 750 million to 9 billion dollars. But it's worth wondering whether a patrimony of such enormous size can be described in numerical terms."[11] The son of a humble postal clerk, at various times throughout his career a telegraph operator, horse thief, spy for the Americans, policeman, military officer, eventually Trujillo became chief of the army and, with the 1930 election, president of the republic. That post soon elevated him to the position of unrivaled master of his country. Trujillo remained in power for thirty years, outdoing Stalin, Franco, and even Mussolini. He had shares in companies that produced or marketed tobacco, oil, salt, beer, meat, milk, matches, cocoa, cement, pharmaceuticals, spices, iron, insurance, and so on. But the conflict of interest that ultimately led to his downfall was about the sugar industry, although the Americans for a period turned a blind eye on it, on account of the Dominican Republic's strategic value in the anti-Communist fight as one of the nearest neighbors to Castro's Cuba.[12]

It's time now, however, to head north toward the United States of America, where, while the noose of terror—and corruption—was tightening in Europe, the country originally founded to escape the corruption of the Old World fell into the worst and most traditional excesses of it.

TWELVE BEYOND THE AGE OF INNOCENCE

*Social and Political Corruption in
the United States through Its Literature
and Popular Culture*

ONE EPISODE OF THE ANIMATED television series *The Simpsons* stages a satirical performance of moral decrepitude that constitutes one of the faces of mature capitalism underlying present-day American society. The motto that appears on the seal of the mayor of Springfield—the pleasant little town that is home to the protagonists, Homer, Marge, Bart, Lisa, and Maggie Simpson—very clearly states the essence of the matter: "Corruptus in extremis." This is a reference to the first citizen, Mayor Joe Quimby, a "model" politician who regularly puts his own personal interests and amusements, as well as beautiful women, before the good of the community. Commissioner Clarence "Clancy" Wiggums considers abuse of office to be the rule, while Mister Burns is the perfect archetype of the bribe-happy businessman. The leading character in the cartoon series, Homer Simpson, inevitably drowns his problems in a hefty helping of doughnuts and cans of Duff beer. The fact that this made-up brand of beer can now be purchased in supermarkets around the real world is irrefutable proof that reality has caught up with and perhaps outstripped even the most paradoxical satirical fiction.

"America was never innocent," the American novelist and essayist James Ellroy has written. "We popped our cherry on the boat over and looked back with no regret. You can't ascribe our fall from grace to any single event or set of circumstances. You can't lose what you lacked at conception."[1] Benjamin Franklin was not only a scientist, journalist, and publisher, he was also a government official in Pennsylvania, and one of the drafters of the Declaration of Independence. He maintained that one of the greatest qualities a merchant and businessman can possess is honesty, not in the classically moralistic sense, but rather in terms of utility. That is, honesty ought to be synonymous with reliability, and if it offers credibility, it can also bring earnings and cash. In short, this describes a form of "self-interested honesty," no longer based on a fragile foundation of a presumed goodness of spirit. Indeed, this is perhaps one of the keys that can help us to orient ourselves in the complex universe of American (and not only American) society, if we consider it as a source of the contemporary wave of e-economy millionaires such as Bill Gates and Mark Zuckerberg who mainly "invest" in charities and foundations.

Mark Twain, a sharp-eyed observer of the politics and society of his times as well as the creator of unforgettable characters and adventures, had an opportunity between 1868 and 1869 to study up close the historic congressional scandal of the Crédit Mobilier. In one of his novels, which bears the unequivocal title of *The Gilded Age*, he assigned to one of his characters, Duff Brown, the appearance and mannerisms of the politician and profiteer Oakes Ames: "The great railroad contractor, and subsequently a well-known member of Congress . . . [was] a very pleasant man if you were not in his way. He had government contracts also, custom houses and dry docks, from Portland to New Orleans, and managed to get out of congress, in appropriations, about weight for weight of gold for the stone furnished." It would be simple enough to find parallels with a number of our present-day profiteers, as we read in the novel how the powerful American shareholder of a railroad describes the tumultuous world of business to a young man eager to further his own brilliant career as an entrepreneur: "A Congressional appropriation costs money. Just reflect, for instance—a majority of the House Committee, say $10,000 apiece—$40,000; a majority of the Senate Committee, the same each—say $40,000; a little extra to one or two chairman of one or two such committees . . . and there's $100,000 of the money gone, to begin with."[2]

But leaving aside the issue of outright criminals (who at least frequently have the courage to openly avow their own criminality), the real problem is that of the protection and cover offered to the criminality that lurks in the nooks and crannies of the political and judicial administration. To say nothing of the law enforcers: In 1959, the New York City policeman Frank Serpico caused a scandal by knocking down the "Blue Wall," long thought impregnable, the seal of silence that had effectively concealed corruption in the New York Police Department. He told his story in a book and wound up on the silver screen, played by Al Pacino. The ensuing investigation of the Knapp Commission, the Italian journalist Vittorio Zucconi wrote,

> tried to distinguish between large-scale corruption and the two-bit variety. It established two categories of cops on the take, as the phrase would have it, that is, paid off by criminals. There were the vegetarians, the "grass eaters," the ones who were satisfied to graze on banknotes slipped into a handshake. . . . And then there were the carnivores, the "meat eaters," the insatiable accomplices of the major criminal organizations, of the gangster, of the Sicilian "*famigghie*," serving them as protection and cover.[3]

At the end of the nineteenth century the conversation began to turn to "social Darwinism," in particular in reference to the ideas of Herbert Spencer and his supposed justification of the unbridled competition and savage individualism dictated by the struggle for social survival. The appellation "Darwinian novelist" was assigned in the United States to Theodore Dreiser, who dedicated a weighty trilogy to the theme of corruption: *The Titan*, inspired by an all-powerful local boss in Louisiana; *The Financier*, which depicts an authentic boss of Chicago, John Powers; and *The Stoic*, dominated by the figure of Frank Algernon Cowperwood, based directly on the life of Charles Tyson Yerkes, a Quaker financier from Philadelphia who tried to take control of the entire Chicago trolley system. Cowperwood is a man without moral or religious principles, incapable of feeling any qualms over the fact that he has, for instance, illicitly earned $2,000 on 200 shares. He simply lacks a conscience, comments Dreiser without seeming to blame him much for it. The "naturalist" Dreiser seemed to believe—at least as a narrator—in the value, defensible to some extent, of a battle without quarter for evolution, a fight that also entails acceptance of the most iniquitous balances to be struck. Cutting out a role as chronicler more than critic, the author wrote concerning as weighty a topic as capital punishment, in a letter about the novel *An American Tragedy*: "My purpose was not to moralize—God forbid—but to give, if possible, a background and a psychology of reality which would somehow explain, if not condone, how such murders happen."[4]

In 1946 the writer Robert Penn Warren published a novel that was destined to enjoy considerable popularity and acclaim, *All the King's Men*, the story of the rise and fall of a political boss in America's Deep South. The protagonist is Willie Stark, who rises rapidly from his beginnings as the incorruptible treasurer of a small rural town in Louisiana to the rank of cynical politician with no illusions, hardened to all moral pressure, ready for whatever compromise is required along his path to achieving his dreams and creating the government of his ambitions.

Warren offers three excellent arguments as justification for the behavior of Willie Stark: First of all, any judgment concerning corruption is rooted in the social class to which the observer belongs, and therefore the ruling elite always finds its own justification, especially among the political and governing class, which willingly accepts the logic of reciprocity when it comes to favors and privileges. Second, corruption is a necessity, and that is particularly true in the career of Willie Stark, who dismisses contemptuously an administrator who resigned out of fear: "He resigned because he wanted to keep his little hands clean. He wanted the bricks but he just didn't know somebody had to paddle in the mud to make 'em. He was like somebody that just loves beefsteak but just can't bear to go to a slaughter pen because there are some bad, rough men down there who aren't animal lovers and who ought to be reported to the S.P.C.A." Last of all—and this is "Warren's third rule"—corruptibility is universal, without any exceptions, in large cities and small towns, in student councils and in the governor's office. In the novel, one of the characters, Judge Montague Irwin, is considered a symbol of unquestionable moral integrity, but Stark has his doubts: "Man is conceived in sin and born in corruption and he passeth from the stink of the didie to the stench of the shroud."[5] In fact, Montague Irwin, a former state attorney general, is discovered to have once accepted a bribe from the American Electric Power Company to dismiss a case against one of its sister corporations. Novels such as *Manhattan Transfer* by John Dos Passos, and more recently, *A Man in Full* by Tom Wolfe, are only a few of the many literary works that feature a convincing description of the fabric of corruption of contemporary society in the New World. With *The Big Money* (part of his U.S.A. trilogy) John Dos Passos, inserting various materials into the narrative, ranging from advertisements to banner headlines from newspapers, offers an absolutely effective cross-section of the manifold and variegated life of the American metropolis through the intertwining lives of men with different destinies, along with a larger picture, teeming with corruption, love, and frenetic vitality.

In one of the most prolific genres around we find at the center of the plot corruption exported around the world by the darkest face of U.S. foreign policy, and especially by the Central Intelligence Agency. The CIA replaced the old O.S.S. in 1947, as the entity overseeing all espionage and counterespionage activities in foreign countries. The organization wound up playing a decisive role in the foreign policy of the United States during the cold war: supporting pro-American regimes around the world, destabilizing regimes that were not considered friendly, intervening in numerous countries to support "fraternal" parties and movements, and not hesitating to make use of illegal means and operations. The CIA is such an "inconvenient presence," even in terms of domestic policy, that some presidents have been persuaded to curtail the scope of its jurisdiction.

Gore Vidal (1925–2012), a grandson of the U.S. senator Thomas Pryor Gore, wrote over the course of more than three decades an expansive series of novels, a seven-volume treatment of the history, politics, and society of the United States that combines invention with realistic documentation. (Vidal decided as a young man not to follow in his grandfather's footsteps into politics, but instead to become a writer.) The last novel in the series, *The Golden Age*, covers the years from 1939 to 1954, from the beginning of the Second World War, which America entered in 1941, approximately until the end of the Korean War.

In *Empire*, narrated from the point of view of John Hay (1838–1905), secretary of state under two presidents,

William McKinley and Theodore Roosevelt, we witness the development of the expansionistic policies of the United States. It is a period that we might well take as a sort of watershed, when the ideals upon which the republic of Lincoln was based transformed themselves in a certain direction to make possible the advent of the American empire. With the war against Spain in 1898 for control of the Caribbean and also the Philippines, the illusion that the United States was an isolationist country vanished once and for all, and was replaced in the twentieth century by the theory and practice of "full-spectrum dominance," which would become fashionable in Washington at the end of the last century. A great many real-life characters appear in the novel: Henry James, the author who denounces American expansionistic policies; Henry Adams, the grandson and great-grandson of two American presidents, a historian, and a symbol of old ideals long since vanished; and then of course Roosevelt, and William Randolph Hearst, the renowned tycoon, owner of a national newspaper chain, a skillful manipulator of news, and a public moralist whose private life gave some reason for scandal in his times. In short, the two authentic archetypes in Vidal's work who incarnate respectively the detested American imperialism and the immense power of the mass media.

THIRTEEN EXPANSION OF THE REALM OF CORRUPTION

From Party Financing to
the "Clash of Civilizations"

ONE OF THE FUNDAMENTAL watershed moments in recent American history was certainly the Watergate scandal. It erupted following the discovery of the break-in by five individuals with links to the Nixon administration and their presence inside Democratic Party headquarters, located in the Watergate hotel and office complex, which gave the scandal its name. The scandal began in 1972 with the legendary investigation by Bob Woodward and Carl Bernstein of the *Washington Post*, and ended with the resignation of President Richard Nixon in August 1974, under threat of impeachment. He was the first U.S. president to resign.

Following the Watergate case, the U.S. Congress passed a number of decisive amendments to the Federal

Campaign Act: introducing the public financing of presidential campaigns, setting a financial cap for individual and group contributions in support of candidates in federal elections, and establishing reporting requirements for sources of financing and election expenses. Since then, the entire cycle of presidential elections, starting with the primaries, has been in part underwritten by the public purse. But perhaps that financing ought not to be public, but instead private and absolutely transparent because—as Thomas Jefferson wrote—there is nothing more odious than forcing someone to finance opinions they do not share: It is immoral and tyrannical.

In Great Britain, the first limits on campaign spending date from the Corrupt Practices Act of 1882, and yet nothing much had changed from the way George Bernard Shaw described it: "An election is a moral horror, as bad as a battle except for the blood; a mud bath for every soul concerned in it."[1] Because, as Niall Ferguson has pointed out, for politicians the costs of election campaigns simply represent a classic example of the "prisoner's dilemma": if the two rival parties were to cooperate, they could limit spending, but the temptation to refrain from collaborating is enormous because the benefit of victory (power) far outweighs the costs of the campaign itself.

And this of course goes as well for corporations and other private entities that support the candidates and thus gain influence: to stigmatize their donations is equivalent to saying that the wealthy ought not to be allowed to purchase more shares of a company than small investors can buy. The "support" doesn't end with elections; it can be said to continue with lobbying: a paid activity in which special interest groups and industries of various hire well-connected professional advocates to propose specific legislation at the Congress—has always been controversial. The term "lobbying" originated in the United States during the presidency of Ulysses Grant (1864–1869), who was accustomed to meeting with the representatives of the various interest groups in the lobby of the Willard Hotel in Washington. The practice found protection in the First Amendment of the American Constitution, which protects the freedom of speech, freedom of the press, and the right of citizens to petition the government for redress of grievances. John Kennedy said that in ten minutes a lobbyist could make him understand a problem that his advisers would take three days to explain. But the need to restrict or regulate a form of representation, however democratic it might be, like that of interest groups, remains quite evident.

James Madison warned in *The Federalist Papers* of the power of the "faction": a group of citizens who are united and activated by some common impulse of passion, or of interest, adverse to the rights of other citizens, or to the interests of the community. To limit their role Madison proposed to make the factions compete with other factions. Since Madison's time a consensus has grown that this competition must be regulated in some way, to prevent a free-for-all, yet despite the numerous attacks on the theory and practice of lobbying by voices of public opinion and the press, legislation to regulate lobbying and lobbyists remained permissive for quite a long time (perhaps as a result of lobbying against a change in the status quo . . .).

Finally, in 1995, the Lobbying Disclosure Act—providing "for the disclosure of lobbying activities to influence the Federal Government, and for other purposes"—introduced some transparency to federal lobbying practices.[2] Further legislation in 2007, the Honest Leadership and Open Government Act, required federal lobbyists to register with the clerk of the United States House of Representatives and the Secretary of the United States Senate. Anyone failing to do so is punishable by a civil fine. But the effective "labor forces" in Washington are probably ten times the thousands regularly registered. Meanwhile, a dozen giant finance, real estate, healthcare, communication, energy, and transportation companies are the real big spenders in the field.

A further risk inherent in the lobbying industry is "revolving door": just as a lobbyist's main asset is contacts with and influence on government officials, the temptation is great for government officials to exit their jobs in the public sector and turn around and start lobbying their ex-colleagues. Successful lobbying can affect not only legislation but also be turned into substantial monetary rewards for the lobbying firms via government projects and contracts in the hundreds of millions for those they represent.

The scandals are numerous. One of the most infamous was the case of the powerful lobbyist Jack Abramoff, whose confessions in 2006 shook the foundations of the Republican Party, which had received an illegal river of cash. The dean of lobbyists, Clark Clifford, allegedly said that he and his colleagues had the right finger to scratch every political itch. But the practice of earmarks that corresponds to so many insertions of amendments and appropriations in the bills of laws, more or less without the knowledge of the congressmen being asked to vote for them, is clearly a practice that runs the risk of abuse.

Certainly one of the most astute strategic admissions of misconduct was the one made by Richard Nixon in a crucial television speech, called the "Checkers" speech, delivered on September 23, 1952, on network TV. Charged by the *New York Times* with having received funds from a number of financers behind his election campaign who had established a fund for his personal expenses, Nixon appeared on TV with a documented list of his earnings and expenses. He added, however, that he had received one gift during the election, and that he had made up his mind that he intended to keep it. "One other thing I probably should tell you, because if I don't they'll probably be saying this about me too. We did get something, a gift, after the election. . . . You know what it was? A little cocker spaniel . . . black and white, spotted."[3] They named the doggie Checkers. The speech, though it touched on a number of other matters, would go down in history for the role played by Checkers, the cocker spaniel given him by a voter in Texas. The refusal to give up Checkers, a number of observers agree, saved his career. Otherwise Nixon's career would not have continued with the momentum that eventually led him to win the presidency over thirty years later.

As Henry Kissinger has said, "I can prove that when I left Washington I wore exactly the same size crown as when I arrived."[4]

One major transition in American history in this field was the legitimization of political action committees, PACs for short, which have become major players in the financing of the parties and therefore power players in the shaping of the national political life. They are funded by corporations, labor unions, and industrial associations. This is the so-called pressure community; associations of corporations, companies, and trade associations that work in concert to further their shared interests, focusing generally on issues of macroeconomic policy and taxation. Trade associations, which represent all the companies active in a given sector, are the essential players when it comes to political action on behalf of business. Trade associations tend to focus chiefly on matters of government regulation.

In Brussels, the de facto capital of the European Union, lobbies are beginning to proliferate and play an often decisive role in terms of influence. Meanwhile, in Washington they have for many years been an authentic power, with an industry-wide volume of business of considerable size, encompassing lawyers, employees, and representatives for each of the individual categories. In addition, there are a great many nonprofit organizations—citizens' groups, public interest groups—that lobby on issues of shared concern that are not always strictly economic in nature. They fight important battles on crucial social and policy issues such as freedom of choice for abortion, nuclear arms proliferation, and racial discrimination.

The work of political lobbyists now extends to and originates far beyond the borders of the country, if it's true that Henry Kissinger and Alexander Haig, like other former secretaries of state, have carried out pressure campaigns in the past on behalf of China, thereby privatizing their public experience. In 2002, the most recent reform, the Bipartisan Campaign Reform Act, focused instead on what is known as soft money, the theoretically unlimited contributions, nominally meant for the parties' organizational activities, that are also regulated with a certain degree of effectiveness. Even George Washington is said to have made a disconcerted statement, at least it has been attributed to him: "Few men have virtue to withstand the highest bidder."[5] The American Constitution, unlike many others, makes explicit reference to corruption as one of the possible reasons for the impeachment of a president. But that does not seem to be enough to prevent purulent boils with planetary consequences on the order of what happened in the Enron case from swelling and occasionally bursting; the Enron case even touched, if marginally, two presidents, George H. W. Bush and his son, George W. Bush.

Indeed, over the years the number of scandals has grown, from Billygate under Jimmy Carter (instituted to cover up the misdeeds of the president's kid brother) to the Iran-*contra* affair under Ronald Reagan (concerning the secret ties between the Reagan administration and Iran and financing for the *contras* in Nicaragua), to Travelgate (concerning the Clintons' replacement of the White House travel office), up to and including Iraqgate. Iraqgate developing more or less in conjunction with the explosion of the bankruptcy case involving the multinational corporation Enron which involved a number of figures in the American congress and executive branch, highlighted the collusions between a number of oil companies and the two presidents Bush (father and son), bringing to light the business dealings of Vice President Dick Cheney, but also the ties existing between the Bush family and the family of Osama bin Laden.

The whiff of scandal was again strong in the 2016 presidential campaign and election. Donald Trump's presidency presents potential conflict-of-interest challenges. He owns more than one hundred companies, with interests in more than one hundred countries, including Argentina, Brazil, India, Turkey, Philippines, and many other countries where the United States has strategic, economic, and geopolitical interest. Some of his companies are debtors of some big banks such as Deutsche Bank and the Bank of China.

Yet Hillary Clinton's candidacy also carried considerable conflict-of-interest baggage, primarily the practices of the Clinton Foundation in soliciting large donations from both domestic players and foreign governments and agents. Certain observers bluntly characterized these activities as "pay to play" with the former secretary of state and, it was assumed, future occupant of the Oval Office.

In 2012 an analysis by the Federal Elections Commission calculated that U.S. senators had to raise almost $10.5 million in order to be able to win or keep their seats.[6] So we can hardly be surprised by the results of an experiment undertaken during the 1996 presidential campaign of Bob Dole and Bill Clinton: A university researcher sent in donations to both candidates from imaginary associations such as Friends of Pedophilia, the Society for the Spread of Cocaine, and funds "for the protection of necrophilia." All the checks were deposited by the candidates' organizations without the slightest inquiry into the source of the money donated.

"There on my desk is a stack of letters this high," recalls the protagonist of Tom Wolfe's *A Man in Full*. "Clipped to each letter is a check made out to my campaign. The letter itself is a contract between me and the organization that sent it. One, I remember, was from some gay rights organization. All I had to do was sign off on this letter saying that I would come out in favor of same-sex marriages, survivor's rights for same-sex couples, gay-sex education starting in elementary school, criminal sanctions against anti-gay bigotry, I can't even remember it all, and I could have the check, which was for $20,000."[7]

Ambrose Bierce, in a short sketch from *Fantastic Fables*, writes, "A Member of a Legislature who had pledged himself to his Constituents not to steal, brought home at the end of the session a large part of the dome of the Capitol. Thereupon the Constituents held an indignation meeting and passed a resolution of tar and feathers. 'You are most unjust,' said the Member of the Legislature. 'It is true I promised you I would not steal; but had I ever promised you that I would not lie?' "[8] Bierce's congressman has the indubitable merit of telling us exactly the way things really stand: The lie is the queen of politics. The real evil, he seems to be telling us, is to be found not in the theft but in the concealment of the theft, in the intellectual dishonesty that comes in the wake of the burglary. And so, perhaps this is really the point: If it is not possible to prevent theft and the peddling of influence, even in a totalitarian regime, then let us at least lay the essential groundwork to ensure that it is not necessary to lie and clumsily conceal the obvious truth.

In a system of democratic representation, the need for private political financing is an inescapable reality, just as the bartering of votes appears to be a rule without exceptions. Consensus is created through the basic interactions of clientelism and with the equitable distribution of favors, because deep down, we might say, it is the rules of economics that govern human relations, all the more reason to note that the bond of representation ties the political class to its voters. C. Wright Mills, in the 1950s, wrote a book entitled *White Collar* (the term "white collar" is said to have been coined by the writer Upton Sinclair, but its origin is probably older), which comes very close to the truth when it describes contemporary society as a "great salesroom": "The salesman's world has now become everybody's world, and, in some part, everybody has become a salesman. The enlarged market has become at once more impersonal and more intimate. What is there that does not pass through the market? Science and love, virtue and conscience, friendliness, carefully nurtured skills and animosities? This is a time of venality. The market now reaches into every institution and every relation. The bargaining manner, the huckstering animus, the memorized theology of pep, the commercialized evaluation of personal traits—they are all around us; in public and in private there is the tang and feel of salesmanship."[9]

For that matter, "Is there some society you know that doesn't run on greed?" Milton Friedman asked in a television interview with Phil Donahue in 1979. "The world runs on individuals pursuing their separate interests." The economist did admit, however, that it is necessary to place certain limits on greed to keep it from doing as much harm as it might do. That is the role of a political and social order. And this, as history shows, is the problem.

It is perhaps also as a reaction to the excessive proliferation of "gray zones" that envelop the so-called costs of politics—costs that, leaving aside their financial aspects, proved increasingly to have human, social, and environmental dimensions as well—that in the second half of the twentieth century, America was the first country to be shaken to its foundations by a wave of protests and demonstrations that targeted consumer society as a whole and the American model of capitalism as a whole. The "imperialist" foreign policy and the corruption of the ruling classes that represented that economic model wound up in the crosshairs of that violent atmosphere of denunciation. A political protest movement erupted that spread through the sixties across the campuses of several of the most important American universities, and would soon reach Europe and set on fire the hearts and souls of an entire generation. The phenomenon would last for years and its supporters would wave their *Little Red Book* along with the texts of their teachers, both good and bad. "The barbaric success-religion of today is consequently not simply contrary to morality: it is the homecoming of the West to the venerable morals of our ancestors," wrote Theodor W. Adorno in *Minima moralia*. "All morality has been modelled on immorality and to this day has reinstated it at every level."[10] Adorno's essays in those years were read alongside those of Max Horkheimer and the Herbert Marcuse of *One-Dimensional Man*, writings that not only show the contradictions between revolutionary principles when adopted by a basically bourgeois class and capitalistic relations between work and labor, but also underscore the ways, in an industrial society, that the principles of authority, utilitarianism, freedom, and hedonism ultimately wind up mutating once and for all the very meaning of those principles.

Aside from the question of just how much truth can actually be found in those thoughts, there can still be no doubt that, a few decades later, the American system and its "neo-imperialism" have once again stepped into the dock as defendants, in an era characterized by a profoundly modified international political situation, given the disappearance of the characteristics of the old system: the agreements on nuclear deterrence that characterized the cold war, the collapse of the Berlin Wall, and the dissolution of the Soviet Union, up to and including the new and ineluctable clash between the North and the South of the world and the explosion of the already difficult equilibriums in the Middle East. But here, too, reflection on the supposedly unsustainable nature of a political and economic model that seems incapable of doing without at least a certain degree of corruption is hardly surprising.

A number of political scientists who have devoted their attention to studying developing countries have noted how corruption plays an essential role in the process of democratic development. One of these political scientists is Samuel Huntington, creator of a popular meme drawn from his book *The Clash of Civilizations*. Huntington was long known, especially in the world of academia, for having maintained, in his book *Political Order in Changing Societies*, that given certain historic and social conditions, corruption can even be considered a factor of modernization and economic progress. For instance, it allows social change to take place and it can be seen as the only way for emerging classes to overcome the barriers set up by the established elites. Political and administrative corruption ensures a streamlining of bureaucratic procedures, whereas economic corruption can be seen as a selection of the principal market actors where only those better able to invest in a powerful and effective manner—in the right bribes as much as in all other branches of their activity—will be able to carry on their entrepreneurial projects. Examples of such a development model? For Huntington those would include not only the developing nations of the seventies but also England in the eighteenth century, on the eve of the Industrial Revolution, and North America in the years of the winning of the West and the building of the railroads.

In other words, the trading of favors, was thought by Huntington to support the birth of political parties and encourage social and economic progress. The reality is perhaps a little more complex. To offer just one example, in 1996 the South Koreans found the former president Chun Doo-hwan guilty of corruption. We should point out that he was not only a dictator, responsible for bloody repressions but also the leader responsible for the economic miracle of the eighties, which led the country to become one of the world's top ten industrial powers. Before sentencing him to death, ought the South Koreans perhaps to have acknowledged his merit in having allowed a formidable acceleration of the nation's economic growth, even as he himself profited insatiably from major public works and ordinary public contracts? This dynamic is in operation not only in the second and third worlds but also, of course, in what is now known as the first world. We have already had an opportunity to point out that in the United States, in the period of its greatest economic expansion—and certainly not only the United States—an essential contribution to its development was the corrupt practices of the political and business class. Some form of kleptocracy would appear to be complementary to the necessary accumulation of capital.

In the age of *The Clash of Civilizations*, the works of
Thucydides and the writings of Machiavelli seem to have
become once again crucial texts for so-called neoconser-
vative and neo-imperialist thinkers. They consider the
blithe disregard of international law, more or less oriented
toward the hunt for petroleum resources or guided by the
powerful cartel of military industries, a lesser evil in the
face of global threats such as Islamic fundamentalism,
which would call into question the validity of the Western
civil and economic system.

In many developing countries with new institutions
and a major presence of natural resources (mines, natural
gas, oil wells) there actually prevails a full-fledged economy of plunder that can at least in part be compared to
the colonial economy. Perhaps more than in the traditional plundering models, the ones taking advantage of it
are not only foreign countries and big multinationals but
also local rulers who are often more interested in maximizing their incomes than in using the country's resources to heal situations of immense poverty. The same
is true for plans that are the reverse of plundering, such as
economic aid: corruption is so deeply entrenched that
economic aid result in more or less the same effect. The
Zambian economist Dambisa Moyo, in *Dead Aid*, a book
that caused an outburst of discussion, underscored the
need to change the policies of foreign aid to African nations because that aid has no effect save to increase the
level of corruption and hinder autonomous local development. Moyo's message is a variant on the adage attributed to many, including Jimmy Carter on the presidential
campaign trail in 1976, that aid to developing nations

consists of taxing the poor in rich nations to help the rich in poor nations.

Joseph Mobutu (1930–1997), president of Zaire, is said to have had so much personal wealth that he would charter a Concorde to take his family shopping in Europe, and could have written a check to cover his country's entire foreign debt. He used a government jet to make thirty-two consecutive trips to Venezuela to transport five thousand long-hair sheep to his farm in the jungle. Jean-Bédel Bokassa (1921–1996), a former leader of the Central African Republic, one of the poorest nations in Africa, ordered the purchase for his coronation ceremony of over 100 limousines and 130 purebred horses. His guests drank 65,000 bottles of champagne served by a small army of waiters flown in specially from Paris while a 120-piece orchestra played in the background.

Sani Abacha (1943–1998), a military dictator who ruled Nigeria, died of a heart attack at the age of fifty-four during an orgy with Indian prostitutes. A few weeks later the police stopped his wife at the airport as she attempted to leave the country with thirty-eight suitcases full of cash. François "Papa Doc" Duvalier (1907–1971; president of Haiti 1957–1971), directly rerouted millions of dollars in foreign aid into his personal bank account. His son, Jean-Claude "Baby Doc" Duvalier, the youngest head of state on earth, managed to lay his hands on $22 million from the treasury of Haiti before the International Monetary Fund tried to stop him. Much of that money later financed his and his wife's extravagant lifestyle that included $50,000 a month on flowers, and air conditioning turned down low enough so that they could wear fur coats indoors. But there have been a great many cases like this one in the larger sphere of the globalization of corruption: in Nigeria, in Zaire under Mobutu Sese Seko (1930–1997), in Indonesia under Suharto (1921–2008), in Iraq under Saddam Hussein (1937–2006), in the Philippines under Ferdinand Marcos (1917–1989) and Jospeh Estrada (b. 1937), in Kazakhstan under Nursultain Nazarbayev (b. 1940), and in Puerto Rico under Pedro Rosselló (b. 1944).

"Corruption is our protection. Corruption keeps us safe and warm. Corruption is why you and I are prancing around in here instead of fighting over scraps of meat out in the street. Corruption is why we win."[11] That is the lesson in realism imparted to George Clooney's character in *Syriana*, a movie that tells the story of a CIA agent and the investigations of the U.S. State Department and a major law firm into two oil companies that merge in order to exploit the rich petroleum deposits of Kazakhstan. That lesson certainly hasn't become obsolete simply because of new international rules or imagined moralistic turning points in the daily conduct of international relations between public and private actors, especially in parts of the world where wars such as the 2003 invasion of Iraq make it so much more dramatically difficult to distinguish between good guys and bad guys.

FOURTEEN CORRUPT FINANCE: THE GREAT MARKET COLLAPSES

Financial Crimes and Misdemeanors from the South Sea Bubble to the Crash of 2008

AT THE END OF THE 1930S, Edwin H. Sutherland, a sociologist, coined the expression "white collar crime," which he defined in 1939, during an address to the American Sociological Society, as "crime committed by a person of respectability and high social status in the course of his occupation." This kind of crime was studied by Sutherland in the context of a research project undertaken on certain corporations—including General Motors, Philip Morris, and Chrysler—that had been implicated in trials for financial fraud, cases of corruption, violations of antitrust laws and other administrative, civil and penal violations that were connected to their work and the productive activity of specialization of the individual companies in question. The Italian criminologist Cesare Lombroso (1835–1909) had noted, in an essay devoted to a number of banking scandals of his time: "Through an evolutionary transformation, fraud replaces the harsh cruelty of primitive man with greed and lying, traits that are becoming widespread and are most dangerous in criminals."[1]

Sutherland's thesis is that there is no natural predisposition to crime among white-collar employees; rather, their propensity to commit crimes was acquired in the workplace. Pierpaolo Martucci observed in his book on economic crimes, *Le piaghe d'Italia* (The wounds of Italy), a sort of double morality forms whereby the most conscientious impulses of the conventional thinker coexist with the inclination to cut corners found in a member of the business community who essentially pursues the objective of maximizing corporate profit. Bankruptcy, accounting fraud, or swindling are clearly viewed as less serious than an ordinary robbery, even though the ensuing consequences may be much more serious. To mention just one example, the petroleum fraud in Italy at the end of the seventies, which involved the failure to pay taxes on hydrocarbons, netted close to 2.5 trillion lire in the money of the time for the Italian state and its citizens. We are now talking about economic corruption, the corruption of business and also finance. There were a great many victims: the Italian state, the citizenry, the companies' shareholders, the creditors, the competitors, and others. Since then, financial and fiscal fraud has only grown more refined and has also taken on a global scale, in some cases with catastrophic outcomes.

Even the economist John Maynard Keynes (1883–1946), who had brilliantly intuited the dangers of the "animal spirits" of capitalism, seems to have been mistaken when he foresaw the end of the rentier and of speculator capitalism. He was wrong, as was shown by the subprime crisis, which began in 2006 and transformed itself starkly into the great recession between 2007 and 2008. The liberal economist Paul Krugman had analyzed the various crises that had economically devastated a number of countries in Asia and Latin America during previous years and had predicted that similar collapses could hit developed countries such as the United States, and that's not all. The threat of a new Great Depression was anything but remote because modern finance had become immune to the remedies devised in the aftermath of the crisis of 1929. And the "big bust" of September 2008 showed how right Krugman had been to worry (Krugman won the Nobel Prize for Economics that same year).

Advance warning of the 2008 crisis had come in 1989, when Japan was shaken by major bankruptcies. It ought to have sounded an alarm, since the bank failures had affected the world's second-largest economy, once a champion of growth in the industrialized world. In Japan, too, as in the United States in 2008, a financial regime largely without rules and devoid of transparency that favored unscrupulous banks, had led to the formation of a major speculative bubble. For years, speculators—through investment funds, hedge funds, and derivatives—carried on operations that defied common sense on risky securities that could not easily be liquidated. The investors who entrusted these managers with their money never asked whether the company was sufficiently capitalized. The leading investment banks collapsed because—according to Krugman—they had never been regulated. The "animal spirits" led to the implosion of the real estate bubble, the run on the banks, the lack of liquidity, and the currency crises, which all took the economy back to the brink of depression, and the risk that free markets might not survive that drying up of demand.

Nouriel Roubini, an American economist of Iranian origin, had studied the crises of the nineties and had come to the conclusion that a critical common factor in financial collapses was a current-account deficit financed with foreign debt. In 2004 he wrote that the United States would also soon be hit by a comparable crisis. "My friend Nassim Taleb," he wrote, "popularized the concept of 'Black Swans,' those economic and financial events that are sudden, unexpected and unpredictable. But if you look at financial crises through history—and the earliest is the Tulipmania in the Netherlands in the 17th Century—you see a pattern that is highly regular and predictable: An asset bubble—often in real estate or in stock markets or in a new industry—leads to financial euphoria, excessive risk taking, an accumulation of excessive debt and leverage. So the signposts of this phase— asset boom and bubble, followed by the eventual bust and crash—are highly predictable if one looks at the economic and financial indicators that show the build-up of such excesses."[2]

The scholars Paolo Prodi and Guido Rossi in their thoughts on the modern meaning of the ancient biblical commandment, "thou shalt not steal" explain: "The present-day globalized thief is not he who breaks the rules of the market but rather the investor who performs dishonest actions while the very rules of the market tend to legitimize him." We are well beyond any new commandment concerning the maximization of profit. What prevails is a model of stock-owned corporations as "coacervates of contracts, actually without any links of continuity joining shareholders, managers, creditors, employees, and any and all other kinds of stakeholders, persons or entities that have any interest in the corporation's activity. Contracts that basically are there to protect only the figures mentioned, but not all the others, investors first and foremost, who remain entirely without guarantees."[3]

In his 1922 film, *Dr. Mabuse the Gambler*, the German Expressionist director Fritz Lang presented an early chilling portrait of the encounter between crime and capitalism. The psychoanalyst figure created by Lang is capable of adapting to any setting like a veritable chameleon, variously at his ease in the guise of a stock speculator eager to engage in fraud (who goes on to trigger panic and losses among the shareholders), a gambler in illegal casinos, a counterfeiter, the head of a gang of criminals, and a subversive populist leader. He is a manipulator of other people's minds who will ultimately be lost in his own nightmares, leaving to us the even worse nightmares of certain kinds of finance capitalism.

"The economy of the nineties was an adulterated cocktail: three parts lies and one part greed, the whole thing shakered by the famous 'invisible hand,'" stated Joseph Stiglitz, the former chairman of President Bill Clinton's Council of Economic Advisors and a winner of the Nobel Prize for Economics. Stiglitz, the author of *Globalization and Its Discontents*, made the statement in an interview on October 22, 2003, speaking at a meeting

hosted by the Italian Democratic Party in Formia. "Everyone was lying to everyone else," he continued. "CEOs were
providing doctored information about the companies
that they ran, analysts were pretending to believe them
while pawning off those enthusiastic descriptions on investors, auditing companies certified this nonsense while
even the Federal Reserve did little or nothing to tame
what Greenspan himself denounced as irrational exuber-
ance. But there was also greed on the investors' part, who
wanted to believe in the fairytale that they could all become billionaires from one day to the next. Too much
capital had been piled up, there was too much money to
be invested, and it all served as an incentive to dishonesty
for all the players."[4] The conflicts of interest of the analysts who were more concerned about getting business for
their employers than giving good advice to small investors are just further proof of that fact.

The Enron and Worldcom scandals offered confirmation of malfeasance and corruption to a startling degree. The alleged conflicts of interests of the American
president George W. Bush in the events that led to the collapse of the multinational Enron and the role of Hallibur-
ton and other American corporations as profiteers in the
reconstruction of Iraq that occurred in the wake of the
American invasion of that country is just the latest example of the involvement of the highest American political offices in scandals of vast and varied scope and scale.

Starting in the 1910s, continual fraud and financial
speculation led to a reaction by the legislatures in many
of the United States, which passed so-called blue sky
laws, designed to limit the damage from reckless financiers who were ready to sell the public "so many feet of

blue sky." The American stock market crash of 1929 induced Congress to pass the Glass-Steagall Act, which among other things prohibited banks from financing corporations directly—that is, engaging in investment banking. The result was beneficial, because it led to the creation of the largest financial market on earth and a system of controls entrusted to an independent authority, the Securities and Exchange Commission (SEC). The SEC undertook significant investigations into the corruption of the American financial system, though without playing a specific role in the fight against corruption. Instead the SEC has made use of its mandate to protect the investments of millions of American savers. Thus, in the 1970s the SEC went after the system of illegal outlays and corruption on a worldwide level. More recently the SEC has leveled serious charges against an entire well-established and extensive financial system that is characterized by auditors' conflicts of interest of gigantic proportions, ultimately dragging through the mud such sterling names as Arthur Andersen and Merrill Lynch. Though that did nothing to prevent the explosion of the subprime crisis and the collapse of Lehman Brothers.

In the economic and financial field, there are still many who believe that Adam Smith's "invisible hand" ought to ensure that when an individual pursues his own interests he is at the same time pursuing those of the collective. Sadly, however, that's not the way it is: An absolute free-market approach is probably as utopian as socialism. A functioning free market requires that there be severe sanctions in place to prevent, for instance, the natural tendency of entrepreneurs to create situations of monopoly markets.

Alongside the economic crimes of the main market actors, we should keep in mind the extraordinary credulousness of the universe of investors, a phenomenon as cyclical and repetitious as it is surprising and irrational, including over the course of centuries the tulipmania in the seventeenth-century Netherlands, the South Sea Bubble in the eighteenth century, railway mania in the nineteenth century, the dramatic collapse of Wall Street in 1929 (followed by the Great Depression in the 1930s), Black Monday in 1987, the financial crisis of the Asian Tigers in the early nineties, the collapse of the dot-coms in 2000, right up to the great financial crisis in 2008, which still drags down many nations around the world. In all these cases, the bad faith of a financial buccaneer such as Bernard Madoff, at the helm of a scientific system of fraud, or of an entire unsustainable financial system, like that of the subprime mortgages and the trade in them, and the blessed hope of easy money on the part of investors seem to come together as if by magic. Isolated cases? Or just a "few bad apples," as some said in the aftermath of the Enron case? That explanation is easily debunked by an excellent Canadian documentary, *The Corporation*, based on an investigative book by Joel Bakan, which opens with President George Bush holding a quite embarrassing address to the nation after the Enron scandal, which involved quite a few members of his administration.

In 1909, Thomas Mann, inspired by the true story of a Romanian swindler, George Manolescu, and the book Manolescu wrote about his life called *Prince of Thieves*, began writing a novel that he left unfinished: *Confessions of Felix Krull.* It is the story of a great impostor capable of standing out against the vast ranks of other speculators and con men. Krull was the authentic apotheosis of an artist of crime, an exploiter of his fellow man, who was portrayed by Mann as a basically positive protagonist, a protean figure capable of deceiving anyone by shifting shape like a masterful chameleon. As a boy Manolescu carved out for himself the role of king; later in his trips through Europe he would variously take on the roles of elevator attendant, waiter, and the Marquis de Venosta, making extensive use of a weapon that is decisive in politics as well: that of changing one's appearance through facial disguises in a way that seems to modify one's original identity.

Likewise, at the turn of the twentieth century, the talk of the moment was the success of Guglielmo Marconi, the Italian scientist and Nobel laureate who became a brilliant businessman in Great Britain (an early case of the *bel paese*'s international "brain drain"): His corporation, the American Marconi Corporation, was poised to take over radio broadcasts and transmissions throughout the British Empire. But in 1912 certain members of the government, Lloyd George foremost among them, took advantage of inside information they possessed and purchased 10,000 shares of the American Marconi Corporation. All of them denied they had done such a thing—enough for parliament to let them off the hook—but they probably made sizable profits from their insider trading. In this episode, Gilbert K. Chesterton supported his brother Cecil, who with his newspaper *The New Witness* was one of those who denounced the double dealing:

A man like Lord Murray pulled the strings, especially the purse strings; but the whole point of his position was that all sorts of strings had got entangled. The secret strength of the money he held did not lie merely in the fact that it was his money. It lay precisely in the fact that nobody had any clear idea of whether it was his money, or his successor's money, or his brother's money, or the Marconi Company's money, or the Liberal Party's money, or the English Nation's money. Mr. Lloyd George has four hundred a year as an M.P.; but he not only gets much more as a Minister, but he might at any time get immeasurably more by speculating on State secrets that are necessarily known to him.[5]

In Italy during the years of the Banca Romana scandal, 1893–1894, in the satirical newspaper, *L'Asino*, this little ditty with universal application appeared: "Try stealing a loaf from a baker's boy—thwack! / straight to jail, a target of outraged bigotry! / if instead you pilfer a few millions / next thing you know you're a captain of industry." And that too is what Emile Blondet seems to think, as he puts it in Balzac's *Human Comedy*:

The thing may look queer on a small scale, but on a large we call it finance. . . . You take five thousand francs out of my desk; to the hulks you go. But with a sop cleverly pushed into the jaws of a thousand speculators, you can cram the stock of any bankrupt republic or monarchy down their throats; even if the loan has been floated, as Couture says, to pay the interest on that very same national debt. Nobody can complain. These are the real principles of the present Golden Age.[6]

The important thing in financial swindles or political and financial frauds, now as in the past, is to win over the crowds with your dreams. That is the case of Herman Melville's *The Confidence-Man*, in which a man with a wooden leg successively dons the identity of strolling vendor, profiteer, and miracle healer, succeeding at the peak of his business affairs in selling shares in a company that may not exist but that boasts an alluring name, the Black Rapids Coal Company. The same mechanism that was at work, as narrated by the historian of money Alexander Del Mar, in the celebrated case of the East India Company:

In 1613 the Company obtained a charter with extended powers. . . . With the downfall of Charles I., the Company was almost extinguished. Its aggressiveness and avidity had procured it many enemies, and rendered it so unpopular that in 1655, Cromwell annulled its exclusive privileges and declared the Oriental trade open to all Englishmen. Two years later the Company's influence with the Council of State was sufficient to induce the Protector to renew its monopoly. In 1662 Charles II confirmed this renewal and, for a corrupt consideration, permanently established this Company of money-changers, privateers, filibusters and bullies. From that year dates a new order of men in England. The Estates formerly consisted of the Crown, the Church, the Lords and the Commons. To these were now added the financiers, or Billoneurs, who have since almost entirely swallowed the others.[7]

Let's take the case of Sir Isaac Newton (1643–1727). In 1695 he abandoned his scientific studies, leaving Cambridge for London to take up the position of warden of the Royal Mint. He did the job efficiently for many years, helping to carry out a monetary reform and distinguishing himself in the prosecution of counterfeiters. He often pursued the investigations himself, lurking at night in some of the worst neighborhoods in London. His most illustrious victim was William Chaloner, a character who rose from poor beginnings to become wealthy and powerful thanks to his trafficking in counterfeits, to such an extent that he was able to exert influence over a number of members of parliament and who, once brought up on charges, attempted to ruin Newton by insinuating that he was guilty of corruption. Well, Newton, like many others, had an unfortunate encounter with the notorious South Sea Bubble. In 1720 the South Sea Company, expecting to make large earnings by trading with the South American regions, attempted to take over the British public debt, giving shares of the company to the government's creditors. Investors, under the joint action of the Bank of England and the South Sea Company (which was in part publicly owned), rushed to purchase these shares, made available at higher and higher prices. The money flowed in until the discovery that the share prices of the company were overvalued. A collapse ensued and the investors were ruined. This led to the Bubble Act, a law that prohibited all joint-stock companies not expressly authorized by royal charter. As noted, Isaac Newton had been among the investors, and perhaps from this formative experience, he is said to have bitterly commented that he could calculate the motion of heavenly bodies, but not the madness of people.

CONCLUSION

A FIRST AND FAIRLY obvious point that we cannot help bumping our noses against from the very start, when we adopt a long-term perspective, is that the phenomenon of corruption is as eternal and as impossible to uproot as it is because it rigorously respects the law of reciprocity, which Marcel Mauss talks about in his studies of primitive societies. In the ironbound law of exchange, every favor corresponds to a self-interested "gift." That hardly means that we can therefore hastily file away this issue of corruption: the mere realization that a disease is highly contagious doesn't seem like a sufficient basis for choosing to ignore it and stop fighting it. Even if all we do is explore the various ways the phenomenon has been practiced, interpreted, and fought over the course of many long ages, it still seems evident that there has been an evolution in the way we interpret and fight corruption, and the way in which it has been forced to assume a variety of different and increasingly refined forms in order to survive.

The moral perception has also evolved. If Aristotle is the founding father of ethics, in Christian teleological ethics, including William of Occam's and Thomas More's, the end is indicated by God and by the moral law that descends therefrom. We had to wait for a clearer separation of secular and religious power before we could see that politics must be separate from morality. Subsequently, we also learned how economics are separate from ethics (that's not to say, as John Kenneth Galbraith has said, that history is a demonstration of how to "separate fools from their money").

But separation is not the same as saying that there is a supremacy of politics over morality. It doesn't mean that politics can happily and tyrannically do without morality entirely, as in those cases in which we see the various Caligulas of the era make their horses senators. It ought not to mean that it's acceptable to dirty one's hands just to affirm the principle of harsh realism. Otherwise there is no reason for citizens to obey the laws while those they elect are blithely exempt from that obedience.

It may prove useful to reread Nietzsche, specifically, his discussion in *On the Genealogy of Morality* (1887) of how morality has more to do with utility than with morality itself, because it springs from the need to rein in man's natural feral instincts and the more general need to ensure the survival of the community. In Nietzsche's view, even the idea of "good" is not innocent, as it inevitably translates, in a social context, into the good of one of the castes that society is divided into—roughly said, there exists one moral for the lords and another one for the servants. Such morally connated concepts as guilt and even purity can be seen, Nietzsche argues, to possess a definite utilitarian hue and to be deeply rooted in that source of all evils, an overdeveloped ego. This is especially true for that height of purity that is asceticism. The moral *Mensch* and the tendentially amoral *Übermensch*, in this approach, seem to converge toward a paradoxical congruence.

Max Weber affirms in *Politics as a Vocation* that it is necessary to draw a further distinction between the ethics of moral conviction, deeply rooted personal beliefs about how things should be, and the ethics of responsibility, the day-to-day dealing with things as they are. The work of a true politician, which calls into question the head more than the soul, consists of a careful balance between the two. But this only thrusts us back into the struggle between means and ends. That is why, in the final analysis, Aristotle's ethics of the end seems at least to have the merit of taking into account the achievement of human fulfillment in a collective context—true also for Thomas Aquinas and Saint Augustine. In short, it is unnecessary to create confusion between ethics and politics in order to understand that in any civil coexistence there must be a political morality, just as there must be an economic morality.

The case of Italy in the late nineties and the first decade of the new millennium offers an illuminating example of immoral drift, useful to examine and study as a negative model but also as a spectacularly missed opportunity to reverse the country's "tradition of bribes" and introduce new controls and regulations against corruption. We are talking about the so-called period of Tangentopoli (literally, "Kickback City"), an investigation that began with the 1992 arrest in Milan of the socialist director of a rest home for the elderly and led to a stunning succession of arrests and confessions that ultimately swept through the entire national political panorama over the course of the next few years. In a series of judicial inquiries that started in Milan and spread all over the country, more than 5,000 public officials fell under suspicion, including half of the members of parliament; more than 400 town councils had to be dissolved because of corruption charges.

Leaving aside the cases of personal enrichment by a few defendants, the charges for the most part had to do with illegal financing of the political parties. The social earthquake at first seemed like it might clear the way for genuine change. The chief beneficiary, however, was Silvio Berlusconi, a wealthy businessman, builder, and tycoon of Italian private TV, possessor of a fortune with questionable origins who, thanks to his popularity as a successful businessman and salesman, the massive self-financing of his election campaign, and the support of his own television networks, easily won the 1994 election and took office as Italy's prime minister. This marked the birth of the so-called Second Republic, which in the nearly twenty years of prevalently Berlusconian government that ensued, replaced the inept party-run machinery of the previous years with a sort of caesaristic regime, culminating in a further worsening—if that was possible—of the level of collusion between politics and business that had been revealed as a result of the "Mani Pulite," or "Clean Hands," investigations.

The situation was made especially serious, according to the political scientist Giovanni Sartori, by the birth of Forza Italia, a "corporation as political party" instituted by Berlusconi that was also known later as the People of Freedom, the House of Freedoms, and more informally the "Party of Love." In 1954, when the Christian Democratic leader Amintore Fanfani was first appointed prime minister, he at least made the symbolic gesture of avoiding the appearance of potential corruption by selling through his wife a modest packet of shares. By contrast, Berlusconi's men seemed not to perceive any practical real difference between the state and the corporation. Although Berlusconi has been barred from holding public offices as a result of one of the many trials he has faced, it remains true that he has never stopped being part of the Italian peninsula's political equilibrium, ultimately conditioning the moves of the governments that followed his.

In the meanwhile, however, everyone seems to have forgotten the problem underlying the grave Italian anomaly of those years and the full-fledged constitutional degeneration that the country experienced: the macroscopic conflict of interests and the truly uncommon concentration of power in the hands of a single person. The historian Antonio Gibelli recalls that the prime minister's personal needs were thus transferred into the political sphere, as clearly shown by the promotion of a small army of Berlusconi's lawyers (Cesare Previti, Gaetano Pecorella, Niccolò Ghedini, and other lesser-knowns) to parliamentary rank. Instead of passing laws in the collective interest, the chief preoccupation of these MPs was to draft laws protecting their client, especially to sidestep major laws still in effect to help him escape justice. A quite idiosyncratic way of serving the public interests, if we imply that the public interests are best served by keeping Berlusconi out of jail—as he himself no doubt thought. Over time court proceedings for a number of charges against Berlusconi have fallen under the statute of limitations: Lodo Mondadori (corruption of judges), All Iberian 1 (illegal financing of a political party), and the Lentini Trial (false accounting for the acquisition of a player for the Milan Football Club).

An amnesty eliminated charges in connection with false accounting for the acquisition of land in Macherio. Changes in the law led to an acquittal on All Iberian 2, and in some cases to a full acquittal, such as in the cases of SME, bribery of the Guardia di Finanza, tax fraud for Telecinco, and fraudulent accounting for the Medusa Film Company.

Proceedings have been archived in connection with the RAI-Fininvest advertising cartel, for the Massacres of 1992–1993 trial, for connections to the Mafia, for the Saccà case, and for the charges of bribery in connection with the lawyer David Mills ($600,000 paid for his silence on alleged offshore companies).

Other potential charges are still valid and proceedings are under way, but the truth is that not even the sex scandals (including charges of Berlusconi's having had sexual relations with an underage girl in exchange for payment) seem to have hit him in any definitive manner.

Future historians may look back on this era and laugh, but the people of today laughed a little less heartily when they witnessed on February 3, 2011, the approval by the Italian parliament of a lie told by the then prime minister,

Silvio Berlusconi, knowing as they approved it that it was a lie, and that a court of law of the Italian Republic blocked the verdict against the prime minister. That day a large crowd of representatives of the Italian people decided to believe that when Berlusconi phoned the police headquarters of Milan on the night of May 27, 2010, to request that the police release a young woman who had been taken into custody after a fight and charges of theft, he was performing his duties as prime minister, and not acting as a private citizen. The young woman was none other than the niece of Hosni Mubarak—at the time the president of Egypt—and Berlusconi's intercession on her behalf was, according to his defense counsel, an attempt to forestall an unpleasant diplomatic incident with Cairo, and not at all to prevent a young woman of loose ways from revealing less than savory details about the leader of the nation. It was a contrivance that, while it may have been evidence of a remarkable gift of imagination, certainly bespoke no real clarity of thought, because it was soon clear to one and all that the young woman, known by the name of Ruby Heartbreaker, and at the time underage, and what's more of Moroccan origin (not Egyptian at all), had been a guest many times in Arcore at the home of the prime minister's alter ego, the private citizen Silvio Berlusconi, to attend the notorious "elegant dinner parties" held there. The first person to admit that the line about the Egyptian uncle had been nothing more than a wisecrack in questionable taste was Berlusconi himself. Indeed, as soon as the reports of the phone call to police headquarters became public, the prime minister declared that he had done nothing more than make "a good-hearted attempt to help a person who was in trouble."

The same kind of goodhearted impulse, actually, that had led him to shower with numerous gifts and full-fledged salaries the many young and lovely guests at those dinners (even while he was standing any of a number of trials brought against him).

Paul Ginsborg, an English scholar of Italian history, has observed that Berlusconi was not, actually, an isolated case, but rather one of those figures who emerge from the world of the service industry, particularly from the finance and the telecommunications sectors, and who use their economic and media resources to influence and, in some case, conquer the democratic public sphere. Perhaps that's true, but even if he's not alone, he certainly does represent a particularly illuminating example of a drift toward decadence and corruption whose repercussions can be disastrous for the "public health" of a nation and its citizens.

Who could forget the fable of Agrippa Menenius Lanatus? A consul of the Roman Republic in the fifth century B.C., he stepped in to halt the secession of the plebeians by telling them a parable about the parts of the human body and how each has its own purpose in the greater function of the body. The sixteenth-century man of letters Ortensio Lando, who also translated Thomas More's *Utopia*, wrote another such fable, less well known but still quite excellent, about *The Limbs and the Seat of the Pants*: All the human limbs got together and decided to become enemies of Mr. Bottom. The famed physician Hippocrates was appointed judge. Mr. Bottom, according to the limbs, did nothing but sit around all day like a lazy slob and was foul-smelling—a receptacle of all manner of filth. The ass in question launched a spirited defense of his cause, stating that he always stood unfailingly vigilant at the doors of the body, bringing forth all the filth that the other limbs and parts produced. Hippocrates, needless to say, finally ruled in favor of the ass.

It's easy to see this as the perfect defense of the corrupt man caught with his hand plunged deep in the manure, who points out that the filth is part of the system and he after all is just helping it to work—only by chance, we are given to imagine, is he getting rich in the process. But there is no justification or revisitation of the tried and true chestnut *Così fan tutti* that can entirely conceal an incontrovertible fact that applies to politics and public life over the past several decades: If there has not been an actual increase in the amount of corruption—which remains to be seen—at the very least we cannot miss its explosion into the light of day. There seems to be a tendency to gloss over a practice of malfeasance prohibited by law but widespread as a custom. Perhaps the idea is that its being rooted in the history of mankind ever since ancient times gives it a sort of crooked legitimation.

The Web, citizen journalism, and increasingly viral technological media at the disposal of whistleblowers have all led to growing numbers of denunciations of wrongdoing and demands for transparency. Those cries are being heeded, at least in part, if for no reason other than the inevitable need to keep up with the times, by an ever larger array of public and private institutions. And yet all this does not seem to have hindered any of the old ways. It's one thing to indulge in online rhetoric; it's quite another to actually change administrative practice and individual fraud. If certain barriers of silence and connivance do seem to fall, involving central governments or the rubber walls surrounding tax havens, at the same time new hide-aways spring up constantly, along with different forms of public and private malfeasance, which tend to adapt to the different rules that have in the meantime been adopted. There is a lack of any genuine international oversight or coordination in the struggle against corruption, but perhaps the outlines of the crime that is being attacked remain unclear. Or the problem might be the genuine intentions of countries with laws and customs that remain too widely separated.

Providing an answer to the many questions asked up to here is unquestionably a daunting challenge for anyone, but not to take on the challenge of the problem of corruption, or to speak of it only with hypocritical declarations of good intentions, are both very poor solutions in the face of a phenomenon whose importance over the course of our history is hard to deny. Especially if we are wholeheartedly convinced that, as the journalist, publisher, and polemicist Leo Longanesi said, the word "moral" should be used for something other than the ending of a fairytale. We may perhaps, like Thrasymachus in Plato's *Republic*, ask ourselves whether we "further imagine that the rulers of states, if they are true rulers, never think of their subjects as sheep, and that they are not studying their own advantage day and night."[1] From time immemorial corruption has gone arm in arm with politics, as does vice with mankind. Weber doesn't seem to leave a great deal of room for the possibility of a positive development when he recalls in his essay "Politics as a Vocation," "Also the early Christians knew full well the world is governed by demons and that he who lets himself in for politics, that is, for power and force as means, contracts with diabolical powers."[2]

Aristocratic tyrants, children of the people, and the elect of a democracy—it doesn't change much. No statesman escapes the pressures of the lobbies, more or less legitimate, more or less reinforced with thoughtful gifts, nor does he escape the temptation to transgress that power, "the ultimate aphrodisiac," as Kissinger is said to have called it, makes alluring and brings within reach. No parliamentarian, however unsightly, remains a wallflower during the grand ball of the legislature; none go hungry during the crucial electoral banquet. No man who possesses or represents power, temporal or spiritual, both in the administration of justice and in the executive branch, in a free church and in a free state, and no one who spends time in the palaces of power can consider himself to be far from the world, silenced by honesty, blinded by disinterest, deafened by grace. The customs, the necessities, the proffer, the money, the court of faithful and faithless friends, and even the innate tension to sin, it all flows together and bends the will of the prince, upholstering with velvets and damasks that dreary room, rich only in gray buttons. But since, in the face of any objective analysis of costs and benefits, corruption, above and beyond any pleonastic moral condemnation, demands a de facto taxation on corporations and individuals that diverts resources from the public good, and since precisely for this reason the present-day kleptocracies tend to have unhealthy economies that do not attract investments but instead favor just a few fortunate monopolists, it may be worth thinking about a possible course correction.

The numerous anticorruption movements that have sprung up in recent decades show that there is a determination to combat the phenomenon. They have certainly done good in India by shining a bright light on the rule of law with the India Against Corruption (IAC) case, beginning in 2011, or in Italy with the Five Star Movement led by the comedian Beppe Grillo, but it should also be understood that they have also almost always shown the limits of a political battle by and large destined to remain a protest, or to lose its bite once the movements in question have become genuine parties, perhaps even with responsibilities for governing.

In light of the spread of the phenomenon across all borders and the need to standardize the forms of prevention and punishment in the greatest possible number of countries, one of the most important fronts in the fight against corruption is certainly the international sphere. In this area things began to change at the end of the nineties, with the policies at the World Bank, which plays an essential role in financing the poorer nations in order to encourage growth and development. When James D. Wolfensohn became the president of the World Bank in 1995, he was the first to talk about corruption as a political problem capable of negatively conditioning the goal of economic development. He undertook a strategy that called for imposing sanctions on companies and individuals— denying all forms of credit to those whom internal controls showed to be guilty of fraud, bribery, or other violations. Since then, more than six hundred anticorruption programs have been undertaken in nearly a hundred countries.

There have been two main directions of the citizen response to the great financial and political scandals of recent years: on the one hand the rise of conservative populist movements and leaders such as the libertarian Tea Party, Donald Trump, Jean Marie Le Pen in France, and the UK's Nick Farage, who was in favor of UK's exit from the European Union, and on the other hand left environmentalist organizations and candidates who oppose inequality and corruption such as Occupy Wall Street, the Democratic presidential candidate Bernie Sanders, Pablo Iglesias of Podemos in Spain, and Beppe Grillo of Five Star in Italy.

In Europe it has been calculated that the cost of corruption is roughly 120 billion euros annually, and five European citizens out of every six say that they are very worried about the growth of the phenomenon in their own country. The European Union has a general right to take action against corruption with preventive and security measures but in fact each country has its own internal policies. Unfortunately, the crimes in question increasingly involve persons and companies in different states who are able to take advantage of contradictions and inconsistencies among different fiscal, civil, and criminal codes.

Many European nations have signed the most important anticorruption treaties, those of the United Nations and the Organization for Economic Cooperation and Development, but some have not yet ratified the Council of Europe's Criminal Law Convention on Corruption and the Stockholm Program. In short, a great deal remains to be done in order to ensure that investigators in different nations can cross-reference and exchange crucial information and data.

The solution to universal malfeasance (if we leave aside the idea of being better than this world) probably has nothing to do with the creation of illusory supranational organizations. Solving the problem cannot be entrusted solely to parliamentary or congressional commissions of inquiry or other such political and legislative institutions, generally reliant on the better impulses of a political class that may be relatively uninterested in denying itself opportunities for profit and privilege. Nevertheless, palliatives and homeopathic treatments of various kinds exist that could come in handy, or at least give the illusion of doing some good. Just for starters, there is the old-fashioned and fundamental judicial form of dissuasion from committing crimes: punishment. Certainly, that approach has the inevitable shortcoming of striking only a few among the many guilty parties and the secondary disadvantage of inevitably lengthy timelines. But it remains, even with all its limitations, one of the few authentic restraints likely to restrict the drift into bribery. No one is talking about giving absolute and uncontrolled powers to the magistrature. Another crucial matter is that punishment must always be certain. It is necessary to be able to bring to justice those who commit crimes, apply punishments and sentences with appropriate strictness, as called for by law, with all due deliberate speed in the determination of juridical truth. Does that seem obvious? Unfortunately, it cannot be entirely obvious if as great an intellectual as Leonardo Sciascia was forced to remind us in his lapidary style that the most effective tool with which to fight the Mafia is always and only the law.

Politics has its costs, and in order to face up to those costs, should politics feed at the trough of bribery? In part, this question is reasonable, and it might be possible to move toward a transparent system of enrolment in a public registry of industrial associations, lobbies, and interest groups of various kinds. This would have the anything but negligible consequence of restoring political representation to its proper course of the so-called parliamentary mandate, thereby eliminating the inveterate habit of delegating decisions (of course, only those that concern some immediate interest of the parliamentary in question) to the much deplored model of corporate bargaining.

And even this, evidently, will not be sufficient: the American electoral model is anything but perfect and it almost unfailingly favors the presidential candidates capable of raising the most money. Hence, a possible reform could begin with a gradual withdrawal of the state from the management of the economy, still excessively bound up with a command and control policy, so typical of many European nations. Without expecting to establish from one day to the next a liberal shadow state that limits itself to keeping an eye on law and order and national defense, we might at least attempt to limit its entry into the world of business and finance to a lesser—but stricter—role of controlling and sanctioning malpractice and economic crimes. The cyclical financial breakdowns that have devastated national economies, emptied the pockets of a country's savers and investors, debilitated companies, and wiped out jobs are of course a perennial and terrifying warning as to the imperfections of a "turbocapitalist" system, left to the fundamentalist free hand of the market and monopolistic interests. But for the state to withdraw from the economy does not mean to let the market run riot. It means preventing the state from managing all kinds of companies and services that can normally be managed by private individuals; it means clipping the claws of the political caste that occupies the semipublic structures, whether they manufacture cookies or manage financial resources. It does not mean that the state must abdicate its most authentic function of governing, or that it ought to refrain from passing laws and dictating rules, and ensuring that they are respected.

We might even venture so far as to imagine that, despite the impossibility of being sure that we can avoid encountering thieves in the street, we should at least hope to be immune to the effects of thieves in the government. Unfortunately, a government that is not harnessed and restrained inevitably tends to develop an omnivorous appetite that leads it to extend its tentacles—through the infinite ranks of its elected representatives and the uncontrollable plethora of the administrators, mandarins, *grands commis*, and public consultants at every level and scale—over every aspect of everyday life: from cradle to grave, from the national airlines to transportation of all kinds, from office to the circulation of tricycles, from athletic activities to cultural offerings, from legislation on the length of bananas to regulations on pets in apartments.

If Greece was the cause of the great European psychodrama that we witnessed in 2015, we well know it resulted from a demented spending policy that in recent years engendered public debts on a Pantagruelian scale. This carefree management is in general the product of a political habit typical of Mediterranean countries—Spain, Italy, Portugal, Greece—that are home to a deep-rooted system of clientelism and that experienced over the course of the twentieth century the rise and consolidation of Fascist regimes. To an even greater extent these countries have experienced forms of defective parliamentary representation, such as *caciquismo* on the Iberian peninsula and the *notabilato* on the Italian peninsula, both of them distorted forms of clientelist government on a local basis.

In those countries, the political choices have frequently been the product of a logic of exchange between the citizenry and an individual representative, and between that representative and private corporations, in a quid pro quo that has systematically led to a flourishing culture of conflict of interest on the part of both citizens and politicians. Was it not actually a form of favor swapping to concede facile and generous pensions for state employees at extortionate costs for future generations, guaranteeing benefits not only to the politician himself as an old man, but also to his grateful voters?

An interesting study on the abuse of privilege published by two American academics, Raymond Fisman and Edward Miguel, examined a microcosm that could be described as representative of the entire planet, the foreign diplomats accredited to the United Nations in New York. They have no difficulties parking on the island of Manhattan: Through the benefit of diplomat privilege, they can ignore all parking tickets. What better opportunity to compare the behavior of representatives of nearly 150 countries? Can you guess the results? Many diplomats from northern Europe were never ticketed; leading the charge in terms of illegal parking and numbers of tickets issued were the Arab nations, countries in Eastern Europe, and Africa (Kuwait, Egypt, Bulgaria, Mozambique,

Albania, Angola, Pakistan). Among the European nations, the prizes for abuse of privilege went to Italy, Spain, and Portugal, in that order. In short, no real surprise. The nonchalant abuse of a privilege does not necessarily line up with the worst forms of corruption, but the fact remains that the hierarchy of unpaid parking tickets more or less mirrors the international index of corruption as calculated by Transparency International. Quite simply, most diplomats tend to behave in accordance with the habits and rate of corruption in the country they come from. A cultural issue, in that case? A question of civil and democratic underdevelopment? Of course not. That would be simplistic. The truth is frequently the opposite and the oldest democracies can well be among the most corrupt.

It is true that social disaffection tends to take root, along with an accompanying culture of illegal behavior, where repeated episodes of corruption have taken place in the present or the past, especially on the part of the political class. A political remedy worth exploring was implemented on a local level in the United States at the end of the nineteenth century and in the early years of the twentieth century, where many cities—particularly New York City—had reached intolerable levels of corruption. The choice was to separate the figure of mayor-governor from that of professional city manager who would be appointed by a qualified majority of the representatives elected for a period that cannot coincide with the chief electoral term limit, thereby reducing their political dependency. A distortion of the democratic rule? Perhaps, as it tends to avoid giving the winner of the vote total discretion in terms of appointments, which would be in keeping with the worst practices of the spoils system and the definition of powers and earnings, functionaries, and strategic operative positions. Since most corruption unquestionably derives from handing out positions in the aftermath of an electoral victory, this separation of functions with political leadership on the one hand and management and execution on the other, with a clear offset of timing and renewal of mandates for both roles, can be a significant step forward. Is this a model that might lend itself to implementation on a national level as well? Probably not. But it could be a lead used to drag a country out of a corruption emergency.

After all, such measures are nothing more than a response to the perennial need in a democratic system to establish an effective balance of powers, one that includes justice as well as information and media, the apparently taken-for-granted and yet deeply sacrosanct channel of information, whether on paper, wireless, televisual, digital, and so on. The mass media ought always to be capable of carrying out investigative journalism on every representative elected by the populace, on every functionary hired, and on every penny spent by the public administration—and, it is to be hoped, on the private scandals and the intertwining of state bureaucracy and contracting companies, between the public and the private.

Naturally certain governments will try from time to time to gag the most reckless and inquisitive journalists, to come up with specially devised laws for the purpose, and to try in every way imaginable to discourage the most effective bloodhounds. But the right of journalists to report and denounce, with all of its downsides, should be fiercely defended because it remains, or ought to remain, one of the fundamental countervailing powers in the admittedly malfunctioning democratic systems that we live in. Is there the risk of the media pillorying of those who are investigated, and then perhaps are acquitted after making their way through verdict, appeal, and supreme court? Is there a possibility of being slapped on the front page, denounced as a fiend, with a rich array of police wiretaps to reveal our everyday miseries by means of inadmissible intrusions into our private lives? It's dramatic, potentially tragic, but still, sadly, necessary. In an imperfect democratic system we need to regulate the excesses of unjustified violations of our privacy but still accept the risk of a transparency that can in some cases be quite violent.

It is not surprising that—absent impartial news guaranteed by a publicly owned radio and television service and in the presence of a press that is increasingly being encroached upon by a progressive economic crisis and an undermining of that press's identity—actors, writers, artists, and draftsmen of various derivations frequently have done their best as tellers of tales of government shortcomings and chroniclers of malfeasance to fill in the vacuum of journalistic silence, offering themselves as messengers bearing the bad news left out of the news reports. In these cases, political satire becomes news reporting on the most inconvenient issues, or more frequently, counter-reporting, alternative information. On the other hand, as we have seen in our rapid historical review, men of letters and men of culture have always performed this function, as have many illustrious print media: outside Italy are the French *Le Canard Enchaîné* and the British *Private Eye*, which in the sixties established itself as a periodical that leveled denunciations against the British establishment on a regular basis. In Italy *Il Male* in its way explored the problematic issue of how to produce satire in the form of news. It would seem, then, that the public welcomes an armed satire that strips itself of the garb of entertainment and dons instead the garments of established power, alongside the branches of the executive, legislative, and judiciary (the three classic branches set forth by Montesquieu). Let us refer to it as the satirical branch. It often falls to the branch of justice to settle the many ills of politics, yet even the courts frequently lack the strength and the resources to judge and sentence the corruption of the ruling class, at least not far past the beginning of the appeals process. Who or what else can undertake this trial of the misdeeds of powerful if not satirists and satire? In this way, what was once a side effect of the profession of making people laugh and perhaps reflect now becomes its principal task: that of "disciplining and punishing." Certainly, there is no shortage of contraindications.

Werner Hofmann has recorded instances of the emblematic historical use of caricature that tell us a great deal about the chief public role of satire: the *executio in effigie* that was still widely employed during the sixteenth century. At one time the defendant, emerging after acquittal from the courtroom, became the target of a sort of marketplace stoning, but in the form of a straw man. We can imagine and partially share the objections: We are in the presence of a sort of public liberatory ritual against the bad boys of the moment, who are held up to public ridicule, a moral cleansing that threatens to take aim at the classic scapegoat but that by and large leaves the crime unpunished and the corrupt custom intact. Still, the fact remains that in a not too Orwellian hypothesis of an un-disputed violation of the law with consequences for the public interest in which the natural judges are incapable of issuing a verdict while the traditional press outlets prefer silence or the rehabilitatory nuance, an illustrated maga-zine cover or a cartoon, a comic strip or a mural, a video on YouTube or a composition made out of emojis, all might be able, given the oblique nature of their form of commu-nication, to state what the powers that be are not particu-larly interested in having said. Naturally, a vine charcoal or colored pencil is not actually going to put a stop to the malfeasance of a potentate invested with some popular mandate. But as guerrilla warfare teaches us, the repeated stimulus if administered with wit and originality (love pat, vicious scratch, or poisoned dart) winds up causing annoyance and, in a few lucky instances, like the last drop, even managing to overcome some given and solid form of abuse.

Speaking of freedom of the press and freedom of satire—but also of the capacity to create and understand it—when we talk about corruption we should always and first and foremost remember the "linguistic question," a cultural problem, or perhaps we should say, a matter of education. Numerous studies show that the rate of corrup-tion is inversely proportional to the level of education. In Italy, for instance, 65 percent of the population is incapa-ble of finding their way in the world of information and news reporting in order to construct an informed opin-ion. This is known as functional illiteracy and serves as clear evidence that it is first and foremost a literacy prob-lem that holds back the economy, prevents innovation, and ultimately serves to encourage the underground economy and fosters corruption. The problem is worsened if there is no new blood in the political class that is expected to decide on the investments in universities and research. In Italy, those investments are at levels of roughly one percent, well under the average for the European Union. Conversely, it is clear that a country can become prosperous and honest only if it begins to invest serious resources on those two strategic fronts.

Anticorruption rules and laws, then, are important, and they ought to be taken for granted in a country with a modern rule of law. But political corruption can be effectively battled and diminished only if we sharpen the three principal weapons available for that fight: an efficient and effective system of justice, a free process of newsgathering and reporting, and criteria of accountability for every act of governance or administration on the part of the elected officials. We can add to that list specialized investigative agencies, reward tools, along with whistleblowing systems, undercover agents, and systematic use of big data. . . . Many countries lack at least some of these elements.

"What should a parliament do?" Umberto Eco asked in a spirit of provocation. "Represent all the movements, the demands, the wishes, the needs, the dreams of every member of the social fabric. And do not real estate speculators form part of the social fabric, along with those who would bribe public officials, subversive throwers and planters of bombs, friends of the Greek colonels, buyers of votes, abusive clear-cutters of forests, tax evaders? They will be represented in parliament by corrupt former cabinet ministers, Mafia godfathers, felonious generals. Someone might reasonably object that parliament ought only to represent legal interests through the election of 'honest' men and women. But that strikes me as a patently naïve objection."[3]

In spite of the proliferation of systems of corrupt power, the most important aspect that emerges as we reread the development of corruptive practices over time, remains, unbelievably, the real possibility that the phenomenon may ultimately be corrected—certainly never outright eliminated, but perhaps contained. Immersed as we are in a contemporary world subject to the dictates of the global market and the near impossibility of regulating the same, we tend to deny rationally the possibility of a reduction of the widespread level of malfeasance. And yet, if we emerge from the pessimism of the present day, we can surely see that, statistically speaking, the ubiquity of political malfeasance has actually diminished over the long run. In fact, there are many positive cases of evolution and improvement in the rate of criminal activity in history. While it is true that every day there are more and more opportunities to loot and plunder our fellow man, it is every bit as true that generally speaking there is also a growing level of attention on and supervision of those responsible for power and resources.

Look at the United States in the mid-nineteenth century. That is the country that Martin Scorsese depicted with such suggestive effects in *Gangs of New York*: a city more or less under the control of organized crime organizations (including Tammany Hall) and the outsized power of a mayor and his satraps, all more or less local. And yet the situation improves sharply starting at the end of the nineteenth century, owing at least in part to the development of a free press that is independent of the political power base, if it is indeed true, as has been calculated, that between the end of the nineteenth century and the first few decades of the twentieth century, the impact of that press grew exponentially.

If holiness in politics exists, at least as an exception, no one would even dream of asking for it as a precondition of being allowed to govern. The problem is always one of proportion. It's one thing to accept the necessity of the art of compromise on behalf of an objective that redounds to the general interests of the state and the collective, as many from Machiavelli to Weber noted. It's quite another to use one's own position for mere personal enrichment.

To those who scolded him for his involvement in somewhat shady affairs, the French president François Mitterrand liked to say that even the great French of the past such as Richelieu, Mazarin, and Talleyrand had laid their hands on quite a significant pile of booty, but that was not why they were remembered by history. Certainly, but this extreme relativism is a bit of a contrived position, and a dangerous one. And the difficulty of finding a medication for the condition ought not to distract us from our intention to battle the disease.

These days we hear people speak about liquid corruption, which extends the meaning of the felicitous sociological definition of "liquid society" first set forth by Zygmunt Bauman, to underscore the capacity of the phenomenon to permeate every aspect of the lives of each and every one of us. Alongside the theft perpetrated by the high and mighty exists a form of "unconscious corruption" for which we are ultimately all responsible if we accept the rules of an outlaw system, because micro-corruption has always existed alongside its more macro-scopic counterpart. The point, then, as with all forms of evil, is simply—simply?—to resist giving in to the "ba-nality of corruption."

NOTES

Introduction

　　1. Coleridge, *Specimens of the Table Talk*, p. 45.

　　2. Morante, *Opere*, pp. 50–52.

　　3. Le Bon, *The Crowd*, p. 121.

　　4. Washington Irving, "A Time of Unexampled Prosperity," *The Knickerbocker; Or, New-York Monthly Magazine*, vol. 15, April 1840, reprinted in *EIR Economic History*, February 1, 2008 (www.larouchepub.com/eiw/public/2008/2008_1-9/2008_1-9 /2008-5/pdf/38-47_3505.pdf).

　　5. Croce, *A History of Italy*, p. 183.

　　6. Homer, *The Odyssey*, p. 304.

　　7. Homer, *The Iliad*, p. 12.

　　8. See Warren, "Political Corruption as Duplicitous Exclusion."

　　9. Carlyle, *On Heroes,* lecture 4, "The Hero as Priest."

1. The Gift in Antiquity

　　1. Kauṭilya, *Arthashastra*, pp. 93–94.

　　2. Noonan, *Bribes*, p. 4.

　　3. Ibid., p. 9.

2. Democracy and Decadence

    1. Brédif, *Demosthenes*, p. 78.

    2. Plato, *The Republic*, p. 110.

    3. Plato, *Dialogues of Plato*, p. 414.

    4. Murray, *Demosthenes*.

    5. Plato, *The Republic*.

    6. Plato, *The Seventh Letter*, trans. J. Harward (http://classics.mit.edu/Plato/seventh_letter.html).

    7. Sophocles, *Oedipus the King.*

    8. Aristophanes, *The Knights*, pp. 111–12.

    9. Plutarch, *Lives of Illustrious Men*, p. 84.

    10. Plutarch, *Moralia*, in Historical Mirror, *The Historical Mirror; or, Biographical miscellany* (Dublin: Whitestone, Dublin, 1776; reprint, Dublin: Ulan Press, 2012), p. 170.

    11. Onfray, *Cosmos.*

    12. Samuel Arthur Bent, *Familiar Short Sayings of Great Men* (Boston and New York: Houghton, Mifflin & Company, 1887), p. 437.

    13. Augustine, *City of God*, p. 140.

3. Bribes in Ancient Rome

    1. Plutarch, *Plutarch's lives of Themistocles . . .* , p. 305.

    2. H. E. Butler, *Sallust*, pp. 46–47.

    3. Tacitus, *Annals of Tacitus*, pp. 304–05.

    4. H. E. Butler, p. 24.

    5. Ibid., pp. 42–43.

    6. Livy, *History of Rome*, 193–95.

    7. Jon R. Stone, *The Routledge Book of World Proverbs* (London and New York: Routledge, 2006), p. 451.

    8. Seneca, *Seneca*, pp. 109, 115.

    9. Cicero, *Orations*, p. 364.

    10. Cicero, *Letters*, p. 378.

    11. Cicero, *Select Orations*, pp. 88–89.

4. The Feces of the Devil

    1. Bloch, *Feudal Society*, p. 78.

    2. Montaigne, *Montaigne's Essays*, p. 143.

    3. Alighieri, *De Monarchia*, p. 198.

    4. Alighieri, *Divine Comedy*, Canto 21, ll. 41–42.

5. Chaucer, *Canterbury Tales*, p. 199.

6. Martin Luther, *Martin Luther's 95 Theses*, Theses 50 and 66.

7. Paolo da Certaldo, *Il libro dei buoni costumi* (Kindle ed., n.d.; www.amazon.it/Libro-buoni-costumi-Paolo-Certaldo-ebook /dp/B00685L4BU), par. 81.

8. Ibid., par. 97.

9. Galasso, "L'Italia della frammentazione feudale," pp. 412–15. See also Lee, *Ugly Renaissance*.

10. Le Goff, *Your Money or Your Life*, pp. 42, 69.

11. Sombart, *Quintessence of Capitalism*, p. 309.

5. *Corruption in Power*

1. Machiavelli, *The Prince*.

2. Prezzolini, *Nicolò Machiavelli*.

3. Montanelli, "L'Italia della Controriforma."

4. Volpe, *Momenti di storia italiana*.

5. Macchia, *I moralisti classici*.

6. Machiavelli, *Mandragola*, p. 9.

7. Della Casa, *Galateo*, p. 4.

8. Shakespeare, *King Lear*, act 1, scene 1, line 57.

9. Marlowe, *The Jew of Malta*, prologue, lines 28–29.

10. Ward and Waller, eds., *Renascence and Reformation*, p. 137.

11. Rabelais, *Gargantua and Pantagruel*, p. 208.

12. Galbraith, *Economics in Perspective*, pp. 33–35.

13. Las Casas, *Devastation of the Indies*, pp. 28–29.

14. Sepulveda, "La scoperta dei selvaggi," pp. 259–60.

15. See *Secreta Monita Societatis Jesu* (https://archive.org /stream/secretamonitasoc00brec#page/60/mode/2up).

16. Morales, *Oracolo manuale*.

17. Cipolla, *Conquistadores, pirati, mercatanti*.

6. *Philosophy of Corruption*

1. Clapiers, *Introduction à la connaissance de l'esprit humain*.

2. Morand, "*Fouquet ou Le Soleil offusqué*.

3. Ibid.

4. Ibid.

5. Blanning, *The Pursuit of Glory*, p. 562.

6. La Rochefoucauld, *Maxims*, p. 7.

7. Diana Henriques, review of *Millionaire: The Philanderer, Gambler, and Duelist Who Invented Modern Finance*, by Janet Gleeson, *New York Times*, July 23, 2000.

8. Mandeville, *Fable of the Bees*, p. 9.

9. Tocqueville, *Democracy in America*, pp. 131–34.

10. "Charlotte Robespierre's Memoirs," *LiveJournal*, "Welcome to 1789" (http://revolution-fr.livejournal.com/27230.html).

11. Büchner, *Danton's Death*.

12. Robespierre, "On Political Morality" (https://chnm.gmu.edu/revolution/d/413/).

13. Condorcet, *Memoires*, p. 22.

14. Chateaubriand, *Memoirs*, pp. 187–88.

7. A Pragmatic Approach to Corruption

1. Pepys, *Diary*, p. 76.

2. Armitage, *Bolingbroke*.

3. Burke, *Works*.

4. Alexander Pope, *Complete Political Works*, "Moral Essays," Epistle III, "Of the Use of Riches," vv. 135–43 (www.bartleby.com/203/145.html).

8. The American Dream of Purity

1. See "A Biography of Robert Morris, 1734–1806," *American History from Revolution to Reconstruction and Beyond* (www.let.rug.nl/usa/biographies/robert-morris/).

2. See Theodore Roosevelt, "Third Annual Address, December 7, 1903," American Presidency Project (www.presidency.ucsb.edu/ws/?pid=29544).

9. Restoration and Decadence

1. Sombart, *Der moderne Kapitalismus*, p. 332.

2. Simmel, *Philosophy of Money*, p. 407.

3. von Schaukal, *Life and Opinions of Herr Andreas von Balthesser*, p. 54.

4. Roth, *Radetzky March*, p. 135.

5. Mann, *Buddenbrooks*, p. 473.

6. See Hansard (website), "National Representation. HC Deb 20 June 1848 vol 99 cc879-966" (http://hansard.millbanksystems .com/commons/1848/jun/20/national-representation).

7. Roberts, *Eminent Churchillians*, chapter 3. Author's translation.

8. Conrad, *Nostromo*, p. 51. Costaguana very likely was meant to stand in for Colombia.

9. Balzac, *Comédie Humaine*, in *Collected Works*, p. xlvii.

10. Hugo, *Napoleon the Little*, p. 166.

11. Pacelli, *Cattivi esempi*.

12. *Lettere di Massimo D'Azeglio a sua moglie Luisa Blondel*, ed. Giulio Carcano (Carrara and Milan: Rechiedei, 1870), p. 493.

13. Pirandello, *The Old and the Young*.

14. Cavallotti, "Lettera agli onesti di tutti i partiti," *Il Secolo*, June 1895 (supplement).

15. D'Annunzio, *Child of Pleasure*, p. 22.

16. Chamisso, *Shadowless Man*, p. 71.

17. Silvestri, *Decadenza dell'Europa occidentale 1890– 1946*.

10. *Parts in the Play*

1. James, *The Reverberator*, p. 8.

2. Zola, *Money*, pp. 232–33.

3. Zola, *Fortune of the Rougons*.

4. Trollope, *Phineas Finn*, p. 7.

5. Wilson, *Big Sleepover at the White House*, p. 30.

6. Dickens, *Posthumous Papers of the Pickwick Club*, p. 187.

7. Morris, *News from Nowhere*, pp. 73, 63.

8. Noonan, *Bribe*, p. 456.

9. Kraus, *Last Days of Mankind*, scene 29.

10. Leopardi, *Discorso*.

11. Foscolo, "Della morale letteraria; Lezzione Prima; La Letteratura Rivolta Unicamente Al Lucro" (Rome: Biblioteca italiana, 2008) (http://ww2.bibliotecaitaliana.it/xtf/view?docId=bibit 000375%2Fbibit000375.xml&chunk.id=d122e127&query =indipendenza).

12. Nievo, *Confessions of an Italian*.

13. De Roberto, *The Viceroys*, part 2, chapter 8.

14. Angelo Panebianco, "Destra e sinistra, la differenza non è l'etica," *Corriere della Sera*, December 31, 2005.

15. De Roberto, *The Viceroys*, part 3, chapter 9.

16. Collodi, *Adventures of Pinocchio*, p. 142.

11. The Great Dictatorships

1. Report of the Berlin Police, August 1935. Cited in Frank Bajohr, "Der folgenlose Skandal: Korruptionsaffären im National-sozialismus." In Martin Sabrow, ed., *Skandal und Diktatur: Formen öffentlicher Empörung im NS-Staat und in der DDR*. Göttingen: Wallstein Verlag, 2004, p. 59n3.

2. Antonio Gramsci, "I Hate the Indifferent," February 11, 1917, *Against the Current* (blog), August 2016 (http://nzagainst thecurrent.blogspot.com/2012/02/i-hate-indifferent.html).

3. Ward, *Piero Gobetti's New World*, p. 82.

4. "I have a family" is the classic Italian excuse for getting away with tax evasion and other petty crimes.—Translator's note.

5. Petacco, *Riservato per il Duce*.

6. Ibid.

7. Piero Calamandrei, "Patologia della corruzione parlamen-tare," *Il Ponte*, October 1947, pp. 859–75.

8. Pietro Badoglio, speech to the officer corps at Agro S. Giorgio Ionico, October 18, 1943 (www.history.com/this-day-in -history/italy-declares-war-on-germany).

9. Ilf and Petrov, *Little Golden Calf*.

10. Amis, *Koba the Dread*.

11. Enzensberger, "Rafael Trujillo."

12. Hall, *Sugar and Power*.

12. Beyond the Age of Innocence

1. Ellroy, *American Tabloid*, p. 5.

2. Twain, *Gilded Age*, pp. 97, 205.

3. Vittorio Zucconi, "Serpico, il poliziotto-eroe ora vive in una capanna," *La Repubblica*, January 25, 2010.

4. Barton, *Literary Executions*, p. 247.

5. Warren, *All the King's Men*, p. 235.

13. Expansion of the Realm of Corruption

1. Shaw, *Back to Methuselah*, p. 57.

2. "Lobbying Disclosure" (http://lobbyingdisclosure.house
.gov/lda.html).

3. Richard Nixon, "Checkers Speech," American Presidency
Project (www.presidency.ucsb.edu/ws/index.php?pid=24485).

4. *The Hour*, May 19, 1977, p. 40.

5. George Washington, letter to Major-General Robert
Howe, August 17, 1779 (www.mountvernon.org/george
-washington/quotes/article/few-men-have-virtue-to-withstand
-the-highest-bidder/).

6. "U.S. Senate seat now costs $10.5 million to win, on aver-
age, while U.S. House seat costs, $1.7 million, new analysis of
FEC data shows," *Daily News*, March 11, 2013.

7. Wolfe, *A Man in Full*, p. 101.

8. Bierce, *Collected Works*, vol. 4, p. 265.

9. Mills, *White Collar*, p. 161.

10. Adorno, *Minima Moralia*, p. 187.

11. "*Syriana* Director on Ruthless Pursuit of Oil, Power,"
Day to Day, NPR, December 9, 2005, transcript (www.npr.org
/templates/story/story.php?storyId=5046449).

14. Corrupt Finance: The Great Market Collapses

1. Lombroso quoted in Martucci, *Le piaghe d'Italia*.

2. Nouriel Roubini interviewed by Ian Bremmer for Amazon
(www.amazon.com/Crisis-Economics-Course-Future-Finance
/dp/014311963X).

3. Prodi and Rossi, *Non rubare*.

4. "Liberatevi del liberismo. Parola di Nobel," transcript in
Italian, *Criticamente*, October 24, 2003 (www.criticamente.it
/2003/10/24/liberatevi-del-liberismo-parola-di-nobel/).

5. G. K. Chesterton, "The Mask of Socialism" (www.online
-literature.com/chesterton/usurers/9/).

6. Balzac, *Comédie Humaine*, in *Collected Works*.

7. Del Mar, *Barbara Villiers*, p. 9.

Conclusion

1. Plato, *The Republic* (Jowett translation).

2. Max Weber, "Politics as a Vocation," lecture, 1919 (http://anthropos-lab.net/wp/wp-content/uploads/2011/12/Weber-Politics-as-a-Vocation.pdf, p. 24).

3. Eco, *Dalla periferia dell'impero.*

BIBLIOGRAPHY

Accetto, Torquato. *Della dissimulazione onesta*. Turin: Einaudi, 1997.

Adorno, Theodor W. *Minima Moralia: Reflections on a Damaged Life*. London: Verso, 2005.

Alemán, Mateo. *Life and Adventures of Guzman D'Alfarache, Or the Spanish Rogue*. London: Longman, Hurst, Rees, Orme, Brown, and Green, 1823.

Alighieri, Dante. *De Monarchia*. Translated by Aurelia Henry. New York: Houghton Mifflin, 1904.

———. *The Divine Comedy*. London: Penguin, 2012.

Amis, Martin. *Koba the Dread: Laughter and the Twenty Million*. New York: Vintage, 2002.

Apuleio. *Metamorphoses, or The Golden Ass*. Loeb Classical Library, Harvard University Press, 1996.

Arendt, Hannah. *Eichmann in Jerusalem: A Report on the Banality of Evil*. New York: Viking, 1963.

Aristophanes. *The Knights*. Translated and with an introduction and notes by Gilbert Murray. London: George Allen & Unwin, 1956.

Aristotle. *Nicomachean Ethics*. Indianapolis and Cambridge: Hackett, 2014.

Armitage, David, ed. *Bolingbroke: Political Writings*. Cambridge University Press, 1997.

Augustine. *The City of God*. Vol. 1 of *The Works of Aurelius Augustine: A New Translation*. Translated by Rev. Marcus Dods. Edinburgh: T. and T. Clark, 1881.

Bacon, Francis. *Essays*. London: J. M. Dent, 1973.

Bakan, Joel. *The Corporation: The Pathological Pursuit of Profit and Power*. New York: Free Press, 2005.

Balzac, Honoré de. *Collected Works of Honoré Balzac*. Hastings, UK: Delphi Classics, 2014.

Barbey D'Aurevilly, Jules-Amédée. *The Devils*. Translated by Ernest Boyd. New York: Alfred A. Knopf, 1925. Originally published as *Les Diaboliques* (1874).

Baretti, Giuseppe. *Dei modi e costumi d'Italia*. Turin: Aragno, 2003.

Barton, John Cyril. *Literary Executions*. Johns Hopkins University Press, 2014.

Beccaria, Cesare. *Dei delitti e delle pene (On Crimes and Punishments)*. Albany: W. C. Little and Co., 1872.

Belli, Giuseppe Gioachino. *Sonnets of Giuseppe Belli*. Louisiana State University Press, 1981.

Ben Jelloun, Tahar. *Corruption*. New York: New Press, 1995.

Bersezio, Vittorio. *Le miserie di Monsù Travet*. Turin: Centro Studi Piemontesi, 2001.

Berto, Giuseppe. *Modesta proposta per prevenire*. Venice: Marsilio, 1998.

Betti, Ugo. *Corruzione al palazzo di giustizia*. Newton and Compton, 1993.

Bierce, Ambrose G. *The Collected Works of Ambrose Bierce*. 4 vols. New York: Neale Publishing Company, 1909–1912.

Blanning, Tim C. W. *The Pursuit of Glory: Europe, 1648–1815*. New York: Viking, 2007.

Bloch, Marc. *Feudal Society*. Translated by L. A. Manyon. New York: Routledge, 2014.

Bobbio, Norberto, Nicola Matteucci, and Gianfranco Pasquino. *Il dizionario di politica*. Turin: UTET, 2004.

Boccaccio, Giovanni. *Decameron*. London: Penguin, 1995.

Bodin, Jean. *Six Books of the Commonwealth*. Abridged and translated by M. J. Tooley. Oxford: Basil Blackwell, 1955.

Botero, Giovanni. *The Reason of State.* Yale University Press, 1956.

Branca, Vittore, ed. *Mercanti scrittori: ricordi nella Firenze tra Medioevo e Rinascimento.* Milan: Rusconi, 1986.

Brancoli, Rodolfo. *In nome della lobby. Politica e denaro in una democrazia.* Milan: Garzanti Libri, 1990.

Brecht, Bertolt. *The Business Affairs of Mr Julius Caesar.* London: Bloomsbury, 2016.

———. *The Threepenny Opera.* Translated and annotated by Desmond Vesey and Eric Bentley. New York: Grove Press, 1971.

Brédif, L. *Demosthenes, with extracts from his orations, and a critical discussion of the Trial on the crown.* Chicago: S. C. Griggs, 1881.

Buchan, B., and L. Hill. *An Intellectual History of Political Corruption.* London: Palgrave, 2014.

Büchner, Georg. *Danton's Death.* Translated by James Maxwell. San Francisco: Chandler, 1961.

Burckhardt, Jacob. *Force and Freedom: An Interpretation of History.* New York: Pantheon Books, 1943.

Burke, Edmund. *The Works of the Right Honourable Edmund Burke.* Vol. 16. London: C & J Rivington, 1827.

Butler, H. E., ed. *Sallust: The Jagurthine War.* Oxford: Clarendon Press, 1921.

Butler, Samuel. *Dizionario dei luoghi non comuni.* Edited and translated by Guido Almansi. Parma: Guanda, 1998.

———. *Erewhon: or, Over the Range.* London: Trübner, 1872.

Caferra, Vito M. *Il sistema della corruzione: le ragioni, i soggetti, i luoghi.* Rome-Bari: Laterza, 1992.

Calvino, Italo. *Difficult loves; Smog; A Plunge into Real Estate.* London: Vintage, 1999.

Campanella, Tommaso. *The City of the Sun. Ideal Commonwealths.* New York: P.F. Collier and Son, 1901.

Canetti, Elias. *Crowds and Power.* London: Victor Gollancz, 1962.

Cardano, Girolamo. *Il prosseneta ovvero della prudenza politica.* Milan: Berlusconi, 2002.

Carlyle, Thomas. *On Heroes, Hero-Worship, and The Heroic in History.* London: James Fraser, 1841.

Castiglione, Baldassarre. *The Book of the Courtier.* Translated by Charles S. Singleton. New York: Norton, 2002.

Cazzola, Franco. *L'Italia del pizzo: fenomenologia della tangente quotidiana*. Turin: Einaudi, 1992.

Ceccarelli, Filippo. *Il letto e il potere*. Milan: Longanesi, 1994.

Cervantes, Miguel de. *Don Quixote*. Translated by Edith Grossman. New York: HarperCollins, 2003.

Chamisso, Adalbert von. *The Shadowless Man; Or, The Wonderful History of Peter Schlemihl*. London: James Burns, 1845.

Chateaubriand, François-René, vicomte de. *The Memoirs of François René, Vicomte de Chateaubriand, Sometime Ambassador to England*. Translated by Alexander Texieira de Mattos. Vol. 6. London: Freemantle and Co., 1902.

Chaucer, Geoffrey. *The Canterbury Tales*. Translated by Ronald L. Ecker and Eugene Joseph Crook. Palatka, Fla.: Hodge and Braddock, 1993.

Chesterton, Gilbert K. *Utopia of Usurers and Other Essays*. New York: Boni and Liveright, 1917.

Cicero, Marcus Tullius. *The Letters of Cicero: B.C. 68–52*. Vol. 1. London: George Bell & Sons, 1904.

———. *The Orations of Marcus Tullius Cicero*. Translated by C. D. Yonge. Vol. 2. London: Bell & Daldy, 1867.

———. *Select Orations of Marcus Tullius Cicero*. New York: Harper & Brothers, 1856.

Cipolla, Carlo M. *Conquistadores, pirati, mercatanti*. Bologna: Il Mulino, 2003.

Clapiers, Luc de, Marquis de Vauvenargues. *Introduction à la connaissance de l'esprit humain suivie de Réflexions et Maximes*. Paris, 1746.

Colajanni, Napoleone. *Corruzione politica*. 1888; reprint, Palermo: Edizioni La Zisa, 1988.

Colaprico, Piero. *Capire Tangentopoli: un manuale per capire, un saggio per riflettere*. Milan: Il Saggiatore, 1996.

Coleridge, Samuel Taylor. *Specimens of the Table Talk of the Late Samuel Taylor Coleridge*. Vol. 1. New York: Harper and Brothers, 1835.

Collodi, Carlo. *The Adventures of Pinocchio*. Translated by Carol della Chiesa. New York: Macmillan, 1969.

Condorcet, Jean Antoine Nicolas de Caritat. *Memoires de Condorcet sur la Révolution Française*. Paris: Ponthieu, 1824.

Conrad, Joseph. *Nostromo: A Tale of the Seaboard*. Mineola, N.Y.: Dover, 2002.

Courteline, Georges. *The Bureaucrats*. Translated by Eric Sutton. London: Constable, 1928. Originally published as *Messieurs les ronds-de-cuir*.

Crainz, Guido. *Autobiografia di una Repubblica*. Rome: Donzelli, 2010.

Craxi, Bettino. *Il caso C*. Parts 1 and 2. Milan: Giornalisti editori, 1994–1995.

Croce, Benedetto. *A History of Italy, 1871–1915*. Brasted, UK: Russell and Russell, 1963.

Cucchiarelli, Paolo, and Ferdinando Regis. *Mani pulite & bocche aperte: le frasi celebri di Tangentopoli*. Milan: Mondadori, 1997.

D'Annunzio, Gabriele. *The Child of Pleasure*. Translated by Georgina Harding. New York: Geo. H. Richmond and Son, 1898. Originally published as *Il Piacere*.

Daudet, Alphonse. *The Nabob*. Boston: Estes and Lauriat, 1878.

Davigo, Piercamillo. *La giubba del re. Intervista sulla corruzione*. Rome-Bari: Laterza, 1998.

Defoe, Daniel. *Complete Works of Daniel Defoe*. Hastings, UK: Delphi, 2012.

Della Casa, Giovanni. *Galateo: Or, The Rules of Polite Behavior*. Translated by M. F. Rusnak. University of Chicago Press, 2013.

Della Porta, D., and A. Vannucci. *Corruzione politica e amministrazione pubblica: risorse, meccanismi, attori*. Bologna: Il Mulino, 1994.

Del Mar, Alexander. *Barbara Villiers: or A History of Monetary Crimes*. Hawthorne, Calif.: Omni Publications, 1983.

De Mauri, L. *Cinquemila proverbi e motti latini (Flores sententiarum)*. Hoepli, 1990.

De Roberto, Federico. *The Viceroys*. Translated by Archibald Colquhoun. London: Harvill Press, 1989.

Dickens, Charles. *A Christmas Carol*. London: Chapman and Hall, 1843.

———. *The Posthumous Papers of the Pickwick Club*. Vol. 1. 1837; Leipzig: Bernhard Tauchnitz, 1842.

Dionigi, Ivano, ed. *Il dio denaro*. Milan: Rizzoli, 2010.

Dos Passos, John. *Manhattan Transfer*. New York: Harper and Brothers, 1925.

Dostoevsky, Fyodor. *The Best Short Stories of Fyodor Dostoevsky*. New York: Random House/Modern Library, 2001.

Dreiser, Theodore. *The Titan*. London: John Lane, 1914.

Dumas, Alexandre. *The Count of Monte Cristo*. London: Chapman and Hall, 1846.

Eco, Umberto. *Dalla periferia dell'impero. Cronache da un nuovo medioevo*. Milan: Bompiani, 1977.

Einaudi, Luigi. *Prediche inutili*. Turin: Einaudi, 1974.

Ellroy, James. *American Tabloid*. New York: Alfred A. Knopf, 1995.

Enzensberger, Hans Magnus. "Rafael Trujillo: Bildnis eines Landesvaters." *Politik und Verbrechen*. Berlin: Suhrkamp, 1964.

Erasmus of Rotterdam. *In Praise of Folly*. New York: Peter Eckler, 1922.

Ferguson, Niall. *The Cash Nexus: Money and Politics in Modern History, 1700–2000*. London: Allen Lane/Penguin Book, 2001.

Ferrero, Ernesto. *La mala Italia*. Milan: Rizzoli, 1973.

Fini, Massimo. *Denaro: Sterco del demonio*. Padua: Marsilio, 2003.

Foscolo, Ugo. *The Last Letters of Jacopo Ortis*. London: Hesperus Classics, 2002.

Franklin, Benjamin. *The Autobiography of Benjamin Franklin*. London: Henry G. Bohn, 1850.

Galante Garrone, Alessandro. *L'Italia corrotta (1895–1896). Cento anni di malcostume politico*. Rome: Editori Riuniti, 1996.

Galasso, Giuseppe. "L'Italia della frammentazione feudale." In *Storia d'Italia. I caratteri originali*. Turin: Giulio Einaudi Editore, 1972.

Galbraith, John Kenneth. *Economics in Perspective*. New York: Houghton Mifflin, 1988.

Galli, Giorgio. *Affari di Stato. L'Italia sotterranea 1943–1990: storia, politica, partiti, corruzione, misteri, scandali*. Milan: Kaos, 1991.

García Márquez, Gabriel. *The Autumn of the Patriarch*. New York: Harper and Row, 1976.

Garrone, Alessandro Galante. *L'Italia corrotta*. Rome: Editori Riuniti,1996.

Gay, John. *The Beggar's Opera*. London: De La More Press, 1905.

Gibbon, Edward. *The History of the Decline and Fall of the Roman Empire*. London: Strahan and Cadell, 1776.

Gibelli, Antonio. *Berlusconi passato alla storia*. Rome: Donzelli, 2003.

Gide, André. *The Immoralist*. Translated by Richard Howard. New York: Vintage, 1996.

Ginsborg, Paul. *Silvio Berlusconi: Television, Power and Patrimony*. London: Verso, 2005.

Gracián, Baltasar. *El político don Fernando el Católico*, Zaragoza: Diego Dormer, 1640.

———. *Oracolo manuale*. Milan: Rizzoli, 1967; translated by Joseph Jacobs as "The Art of Worldly Wisdom," 1892 (www .monadnock.net/gracian/wisdom.html).

Greene, Robert. *The 48 Laws of Power*. New York: Viking, 1998.

Guazzo, Stefano. *La civil conversazione*. Modena: Panini Franco Cosimo, 1993.

Guerri, Giordano Bruno. *Antistoria degli italiani*. Milan: Mondadori, 1999.

Guicciardini, Francesco. *Ricordi*. Palermo: Mursia, 1994.

Hall, Michael R. *Sugar and Power in the Dominican Republic*. Westport, Conn.: Greenwood, 2000.

Hardy, Thomas. *The Mayor of Casterbridge: A Story of a Man of Character*. London: Sampson, Low, Marston, Searle and Rivington, 1887.

Hazlitt, William. "On the Ignorance of the Learned." *Table-Talk, Essays on Men and Manners*. London: John Warren, 1822.

Hesiod. *Works and Days*. Berkeley: University of California Press, 1996.

Hobbes, Thomas. *Leviathan*. Cambridge University Press, 1904.

Holbach, Paul H.T. d'. *Saggio sull'arte di strisciare ad uso dei Cortigiani*. Translated by E. Schiano di Pepe. Genoa: Il Melangolo, 2009.

Homer. *The Iliad of Homer*. Translated by Samuel Butler. New York: Longmans Green, New York, 1898.

———. *The Odyssey of Homer*. Translated by S. H. Butcher and A. Lang. London: Macmillan, 1879.

Horace (Quintus Horatius Flaccus). *Satires*. New York: Norton, 1977.

Hugo, Victor. *Napoleon the Little*. New York: Howard Fertig, 1992.

Huntington, Samuel P. *The Clash of Civilizations and the Remaking of World Order*. New York: Simon and Schuster, 1996.

Ilf, Ilya, and Evgeny Petrov. *The Little Golden Calf*. Translated by Anne O. Fisher. Montpelier, Vt.: Russian Life Books, 200p.

Incisa di Camerana, Ludovico. *I caudillos. Biografia di un continente*. Milan: Corbaccio, 1994.

James, Henry. *The Reverberator*. London: Macmillan, 1888.

Jonson, Ben. *Volpone and Other Plays*. London: Penguin, 2004.

Jouvenel, Bertrand de. *On Power: The Natural History of Its Growth*. New York: Viking Press, 1948.

Jünger, Ernst. *Rivarol*. Frankfurt am Main: Vittorio Klostermann Verlag, 1956.

Juvenal, Decimus Junius. *Satires*. Oxford: Oxford University Press, 1999.

Kauṭilya, Chanakya. *Arthashastra*. Translated by R. Shamasastry. Bangalore: Government Press, 1915.

Koenig, Gaspard. *Les discrètes vertus de la corruption*. Paris: Grasset, 2009.

Kraus, Karl. *The Last Days of Mankind*. Yale University Press, 2015.

La Boétie, Étienne de. *The Politics of Obedience: The Discourse of Voluntary Servitude*. Translated by Harry Kurz. Montreal, New York, and London: Black Rose Books, 1997.

La Bruyère, Jean de. *The Characters*. London: John C. Nimmo, 1885.

La Fontaine, Jean de. *The Complete Fables of Jean de La Fontaine*. University of Illinois Press, 2007.

La Rochefoucauld, François de. *La Rochefoucauld Maxims*. Mineola, N.Y.: Dover, 2006.

Las Casas, Bartolomé de. *The Devastation of the Indies: A Brief Account*. Translated by Herma Briffault. Johns Hopkins University Press, 1992.

Latouche, Henri de. *L'album perduto*. Milan: Adelphi, 1998.

Le Bon, Gustave. *The Crowd: A Study of the Popular Mind.* London: T. Fisher Unwin, 1910.

Le Goff, Jacques. *Your Money or Your Life: Economy and Religion in the Middle Ages.* Translated by Patricia Ranum. New York: Zone Books, 1988.

Le Roy Ladurie, Emmanuel. *Money, Love, and Death in the Pays d'Oc.* Translated by Alan Sheridan. Harmondsworth, UK: Peregrine, 1984.

Lee, Alexander. *The Ugly Renaissance: Sex, Greed, Violence, and Depravity in an Age of Beauty.* Part 2. London: Doubleday, 2013.

Leopardi, Giacomo. *Discorso sopra lo stato presente dei costumi degl'italiani.* 1824; Milan: Rizzoli, 2003.

Levi, Carlo. *The Watch.* New York: Farrar, Straus and Young, 1951.

Livy. *History of Rome.* Translated by Alfred Cary Schlesinger and Russel Mortimer Geer. Harvard University Press, 1987.

Locke, John. *Two Treatises of Government.* London: Awnsham Churchill, 1689.

Lucian of Samosata. *Lucian's Dialogues.* Translated by Howard Williams. London: George Bell and Sons, 1888.

Luther, Martin. *Martin Luther's 95 Theses: With the Pertinent Documents from the History of the Reformation.* St. Louis, Mo.: Concordia Publishing House, 2004.

Macchia, Giovanni, ed. *I moralisti classici. Da Machiavelli a La Bruyère.* Milan: Adelphi, 1988.

Machiavelli, Niccoló. *The Prince.* Translated by Luigi Ricci. London: Grant Richards, 1903.

———. *Mandragola.* Edited by Pasqua le Stoppelli. Rome: Bulzoni, 2005; translation by Nerida Newbigin, 2009 (www-personal.usyd.edu.au/~nnew4107/Texts/Sixteenth-century_Florence_files/Mandragola_Translation.pdf).

Mackay, Charles. *Extraordinary Popular Delusions and the Madness of Crowds.* London: Richard Bentley, 1841.

Magatti, Mauro. *Corruzione politica e società italiana.* Bologna: Il Mulino, 1996.

Mandeville, Bernard de. *The Fable of the Bees.* London: T. Ostell, 1806.

Manganelli, Giorgio. *Encomio del tiranno. Scritto all'unico scopo di fare dei soldi*. Milan: Adelphi, 1990.

Mann, Thomas. *Buddenbrooks*. Translated by John E. Woods. New York: Vintage Press, 1994.

Manzoni, Alessandro. *Storia della colonna infame*. Milan: Rizzoli, 2002.

Maranini, Giuseppe. *Storia del potere in Italia (1848–1967)*. Milan: Corbaccio, 1995.

Marlowe, Christopher. *Marlowe: Complete Plays*. London: Weidenfeld and Nicolson, 2012.

Marsilio da Padova (Marsilius of Padua), *The Defender of Peace*. Cambridge University Press, 2005.

Martucci, Pierpaolo. *La criminalità economica*. Rome-Bari: Laterza, 2006.

———. *Le piaghe d'Italia. I lombrosiani e I grandi crimini economici nell'Europa di fine Ottocento*. Milan: FrancoAngeli, 2002.

Marx, Karl. *Economic and Philosophic Manuscripts of 1844*. Mineola, N.Y.: Dover, 2007.

Marx, Karl, and Friedrich Engels. *The German Ideology: Including Theses on Feuerbach and Introduction to The Critique of Political Economy*. Amherst, N.Y.: Prometheus Books, 1998.

Maupassant, Guy de. *Bel-Ami*. London: Penguin Classics, 1975.

Mauss, Marcel. *The Gift: Forms and Functions of Exchange in Archaic Societies*. London: Cohen and West, 1966.

Mazarin, Jules (Giulio Mazzarino). *Breviario dei politici secondo il cardinale Mazzarino*. Edited by G. Macchia. Milan: Rizzoli, 2000.

Meredith, George. *The Egoist*. London: Kegan Paul and Co., 1879.

Messina, Sebastiano. *Nomenklatura: come sopravvive in Italia la specie politica piú antica del mondo*. Milan: Mondadori, 1992.

Mills, C. Wright. *White Collar: The American Middle Classes*. Oxford University Press, 2002.

Mongini, R. *Gli impuniti: storie di ordinaria corruzione*. Milan: Sperling and Kupfer, 1992.

Montaigne, Michel de. *Montaigne's Essays and Selected Writings*. Translated and edited by Donald M. Frame. Book 2. New York: St. Martin's Press, 1963.

Montanelli, Indro, and Roberto Gervasso. *L'Italia della Controriforma: 1492–1600*. Vol. 4 of *Storia d'Italia*. Milan: Rizzoli, 2010.

Montesquieu, Charles L. de. *Persian Letters*. Oxford University Press, 2008.

Morand, Paul. *Fouquet ou Le Soleil offusqué*. Paris: Gallimard, 1961.

Morante, Elsa. *Opere*. Vol. 1. Milan: Mondadori/I Meridiani, 1988.

More, Thomas. *Utopia*. Mineola, N.Y.: Dover, 1997.

Morris, William. *News from Nowhere*. London: Longmans, Green, and Co., 1908.

Multatuli (pen name of Eduard Douwes Dekker). *Max Havelaar: Or the Coffee Auctions of the Dutch Trading Company*. Edinburgh: Edmonston and Douglas, 1868.

Murray, A. T., trans. *Demosthenes*. Harvard University Press, 1939.

Musil, Robert. *The Man without Qualities*. New York: Vintage, 1996.

Nencini, Riccardo. *Corrotti e corruttori nel tempo antico*. Florence: Loggia de' Lanzi, 1996.

Nietzsche, Friedrich W. *Beyond Good and Evil: Prelude to a Philosophy of the Future*. Mineola, New York: Dover, 1997.

———. *Ecce Homo: How One Becomes What One Is*. New York: Dover, 2004.

Nievo, Ippolito. *Confessions of an Italian*. London: Penguin, 2014.

Noonan, John T. *Bribe*. University of California Press, 1989.

Olson, Mancur. *Outgrowing Communist and Capitalist Dictatorships*. 1932; New York: Basic Books, 2000.

Onfray, Michael. *Cosmos. Une ontologie matérialiste*. Paris: Flammarion, 2015.

Ortega y Gasset, José. *The Revolt of the Masses*. New York: Norton, 1994.

Orwell, George. *Animal Farm*. London: Secker and Warburg, 1945.

Pacelli, Mario. *Cattivi esempi*. Palermo: Sellerio, 2001.

Pansa, Giampaolo. *Il malloppo*. Milan: Rizzoli, 1989.

Parris, Matthew. *Great Parliamentary Scandals: Four Centuries of Calumny, Smear and Innuendo*. London: Robson Books, 1995.

Pascal, Blaise. *Pensées*. London: Penguin, 1966.

Pepys, Samuel. *The Diary of Samuel Pepys: For the First Time Fully Transcribed from the Shorthand Manuscript*. London: Mynors Bright, Richard Griffin Baron Braybrooke, George Bell and Sons, 1899.

Perelli, Luciano. *La corruzione politica nell'antica Roma*. Milan: Rizzoli, 1999.

Petacco, Arigo. *Riservato per il Duce*. Milan: Mondadori, 1979.

Petrarch (Francesco Petrarca). *Lettere disperse*. Milan: Guanda, 1993.

Petronius Arbiter. *Satyricon*. Loeb Classical Library. Harvard University Press, 1913.

Pirandello, Luigi. *The Oil Jar and Other Stories*. Mineola, N.Y.: Dover, 1995.

Plato. *The Republic*. Translated by Benjamin Jowett. Project Gutenberg, 2016 (http://www.gutenberg.org/files/1497/1497-h /1497-h.htm).

———. *The Republic*. Edited by G. R. F. Ferrari and translated by Tom Griffith. Cambridge University Press, 2000.

———. *The Dialogues of Plato*. Vol. 1. Translated by Benjamin Jowett. 1892; reprint, New York: Random House, 1920.

———. *The Apology, Phædo and Crito*. Harvard Classics, Vol. 2, Part 1. New York: P. F. Collier and Son, 1909–1914.

Plutarch. *Moralia*. Vol. 2, *How to Profit by One's Enemies*. Loeb Classical Library. Harvard University Press, 1928.

———. *Parallel Lives*. Loeb Classical Library. Harvard University Press, 1919.

———. *Plutarch's Lives of Illustrious Men*. Translated by A. H. Clough. Boston: Little, Brown and Co., 1881.

———. *Plutarch's lives of Themistocles, Pericles, Aristides, Alcibiades, and Coriolanus, Demosthenes, and Cicero, Caesar and Anthony*. Edited by Charles W. Eliot, translated by John Dryden, corrected and revised by Arthur Hugh Clough. New York: P. F. Collier, 1909.

———. *Precepts of Statecraft; Moralia*. Vol. 10, *How to Profit by One's Enemies*. Loeb Classical Library. Harvard University Press, 1936.

Popper, Karl R. *The Open Society and Its Enemies*. Princeton University Press, 2013.

Prezzolini, Giuseppe. *Codice della vita italiana*. Turin: Biblioteca del Vascello, 1993.

———. *Nicolò Machiavelli, the Florentine*. Translated by Ralph Roeder. New York: Brentano's, 1928.

Prodi, Paolo, and Guido Rossi. *Non rubare*. Bologna: Il Mulino, 2010.

———. *Dreams*. New York: Barron's Educational Series, 1976.

Rabelais, François. *Five Books of the Lives, Heroic Deeds and Sayings of Gargantua and Pantagruel*. Translated by Thomas Urquhart and Peter Anthony Motteux. Vol. 3. London: A. H. Bullen, 1904.

Ramoneda, Josep. *Después de la pasión política*. Madrid: Taurus, 1999.

Reventlow, Franziska zu. *Der Geldkomplex*. Munich: Langen, 1916.

Ritter, Gerhard. *Die Dämonie der Macht, Betrachtungen über Geschichte und Wesen des Machtproblems im politischen Denken der Neuzeit*. Stuttgart: Heinrich F. C. Hannsmann, 1947.

Riva, Valerio. *Oro da Mosca. I finanziamenti sovietici al Pci dalla Rivoluzione d'ottobre al crollo dell'Urss. Con 240 documenti inediti dagli archivi moscoviti*. Milan: Mondadori, 2002.

Roberts, Andrew. *Eminent Churchillians*. Paris: Hachette, 2010.

Romano, Sergio. *Le Italie parallele. Perché l'Italia non riesce a diventare un paese moderno*. Milan: TEA, 1998.

Rossi, Guido. *Il conflitto epidemico*. Milan: Adelphi, 2003.

Roth, Joseph. *The Radetzky March*. Translated by Joachim Neugroschel. New York: Overlook Press, 1995.

Rousseau, Jean-Jacques. *On the Social Contract*. London: J. M. Dent, 1913.

Ruffolo, Giorgio. *Lo specchio del diavolo*. Turin: Einaudi, 2006.

Salvi, Cesare, and Massimo Villone. *Il costo della democrazia. Eliminare sprechi, clientele e privilegi per riformare la politica*. Milan: Mondadori, 2007.

Sapelli, Giulio. *Cleptocrazia: il meccanismo unico della corruzione tra economia e politica*. Milan: Feltrinelli, 1994.

Saviano, Roberto. *Gomorrah*. New York: Farrar, Straus and Giroux, 2007.

Savona, Ernesto U., and Laura Mezzanotte. *La corruzione in Europa*. Rome: Carocci, 1998.

Scalfari, E., and G. Turani. *Razza padrona*. Milan: Feltrinelli, 1974.

Scamuzzi, Sergio, ed. *Italia illegale*. Turin: Rosemberger and Sellier, 1996.

Sciascia, Leonardo. *La corda pazza. Scrittori e cose della Sicilia*. Milan: Adelphi, 1991.

Seneca, Lucius Annaeus. *Epistulae morales ad Lucilium/Moral Letters to Lucilius*. Loeb Classics. Harvard University Press, 1920.

Sepulveda, Juan Ginès de. *La scoperta dei selvaggi*. Milan: Principato, 1971.

———. *Seneca*. Vol. 6. Harvard University Press, 2006.

Shakespeare, William. *The Riverside Shakespeare*. Complete works. 2nd ed. Boston: Houghton Mifflin, 1997.

Shaw, George Bernard. *Back to Methuselah: A Metabiological Pentateuch*. New York: Brentano's, 1921.

Silj, Alessandro. *Malpaese: Criminalità, corruzione e politica nell'Italia della prima Repubblica*. Rome: Donzelli, 1994.

Silvestri, Mario. *La decadenza dell'Europa Occidentale 1890–1946*. Milan: Rizzoli, 2002.

Simmel, Georg. *The Philosophy of Money*. London and New York: Routledge, 1978.

Smith. Adam, *The Wealth of Nations*. London: W. Strahan and T. Cadell, 1776.

Sombart, Werner. *Der moderne Kapitalismus*. Leipzig: Duncker & Humblot, 1902.

———. *The Quintessence of Capitalism: A Study of the History and Psychology of the Modern Business Man*. New York: E. P. Dutton, 1915.

Sophocles. *Oedipus the King*. Translated and with an introduction by David Grene. University of Chicago Press, 2010.

Spengler, Oswald. *The Decline of the West*. New York: Alfred A. Knopf, 1927.

Stella, Gian Antonio, and Sergio Rizzo. *La casta*. Milan: Rizzoli, 2007.

Stengel, Richard. *You're Too Kind: A Brief History of Flattery.* New York: Simon and Schuster, 2000.

Sterne, Laurence. *The Life and Opinions of Tristram Shandy, Gentleman.* London: Methuen, 1894.

Stiglitz, Joseph E. *Globalization and Its Discontents.* New York: Norton, 2002.

Sullivan, Edwin H. *White Collar Crime.* New York: Holt, Rinehart and Winston, 1949.

Swift, Jonathan. *The Writings of Jonathan Swift: Authoritative Texts, Backgrounds, Criticism.* Edited by Robert A. Greenberg and William B. Piper. New York: Norton, 1973.

Tacitus, Publius Cornelius. *Annals of Tacitus.* Translated by Alfred John Church and William Jackson Broadribb. London: Macmillan, 1921.

———. *Histories.* Rome: W. Heinemann, 1925.

Teachout, Zephyr. *Corruption in America.* Harvard University Press, 2014.

Teodori, Massimo. *Soldi and partiti: quanto costa la democrazia in Italia?* Florence: Ponte alle Grazie, 1999.

Thackeray, William M. *Vanity Fair: A Novel without a Hero.* London: Bradbury and Evans, 1848.

Theophrastus. *Characters.* Boston: Frederic S. Hill, 1881.

Tocqueville, Alexis de. *Democracy in America and Two Essays on America.* New York: Penguin Classics, 2003.

Travaglio, Marco. *Il manuale del perfetto impunito.* Milan: Garzanti Libri, 2000.

Trollope, Anthony. *The Prime Minister.* London: Chapman and Hall, 1876.

Turone, Sergio. *Politica ladra. Storia della corruzione in Italia (1861–1992).* Rome-Bari: Laterza, 1993.

Twain, Mark. *The Gilded Age and Other Stories,* Hartford: American Publishing Company, 1873.

———. *The Man that Corrupted Hadleyburg.* New York: Harper and Brothers, 1900.

Vargas Llosa, Mario. *The Feast of the Goat.* London: Picador, 2001.

Vauvenargues, Luc de Clapiers, marquis de. *Selections from the Characters, Reflexions and Maxims.* Westminster, UK: Archibald Constable, 1903.

Vidal, Gore. *The Golden Age*. New York: Doubleday, 2000.

———. *Empire*. New York: Random House, 1987.

Virgil. *Aeneid*. Loeb Classical Library. Harvard University Press, 2001.

von Schaukal, Richard. *Life and Opinions of Herr Andreas von Balthesser, Dandy and Dilettante*. Translated by Name Michael Kane and Florian Krobb. Riverside, Calif.: Ariadne Press, 2002. Originally published as *Leben und Meinungen des Herrn Andreas von Balthesser eines Dandy und Dilettanten* (Munich: Georg Müller, 1907).

Ward, A., and A. R. Waller, eds. *Renascence and Reformation. The Cambridge History of English Literature*. Vol. 3. New York: Putnam's Sons, 1911.

Ward, David. *Piero Gobetti's New World: Antifascism, Liberalism, Writing*. University of Toronto Press, 2010.

Warren, Mark E. "Political Corruption as Duplicitous Exclusion." *PS: Politics and Science* 39, no. 4 (October 2006): 803–07.

Warren, Robert Penn. *All the King's Men*. New York: Harcourt, Brace, 1946.

Waugh, Evelyn. *Scoop*. Boston: Little, Brown, 1938.

Weber, Max. *The Protestant Ethic and the Spirit of Capitalism*. London: Allen and Unwin, 1930.

Wilson, Angus, and others. *The Seven Deadly Sins*. New York, William Morrow, 1962.

Wilson, James Mikel. *The Big Sleepover at the White House*. Columbus, Ohio: Gatekeeper Press, 2015.

Wolfe, Tom. *A Man in Full*. New York: Farrar, Straus and Giroux, 1998.

Yourcenar, Marguerite. *Œuvres romanesques*. Paris: Gallimard, 1991.

Zakaria, Fareed. *The Future of Freedom: Illiberal Democracy at Home and Abroad*. New York: Norton, 2003.

Zola, Émile. *The Fortune of the Rougons*. Translated by Brian Nelson. 1871; reprint, Oxford University Press, 2012.

———. *Money*. Translated by Alfred Vizetelly. New York: Mondial, 2007.

INDEX